Vikram Seth's Art

AN APPRAISAL

Vikram Seth's Art

AN APPRAISAL

Roopali Gupta

ATLANTIC®

PUBLISHERS & DISTRIBUTORS

Published by
ATLANTIC®
PUBLISHERS & DISTRIBUTORS
B-2, Vishal Enclave, Opp. Rajouri Garden,
New Delhi-110027
Phones : 25413460, 25429987, 25466842

Sales Office
7/22, Ansari Road, Darya Ganj,
New Delhi-110002
Phones : 23273880, 23275880, 23280451
Fax : 91-11-23285873
web : www.atlanticbooks.com
e-mail : info@atlanticbooks.com

ISBN 81-269-0550-6

Printed in India
at Nice Printing Press, Delhi

Preface

For too many years, we have missed the pleasure of rhythm in writing. The prose writers seem to have forgotten how to infuse their works with poetic expressions, and the poets have forgotten how to relate a story. Vikram Seth, one of the great literary artists of the modern age, has broken new ground by skilfully incorporating both these elements into his art. The author of two novels in prose, a novel in verse, four collections of poetry, a book of children's fables in verse, a libretto and a travelogue, Seth has emerged as an artist whose creativity finds expression in diverse literary media, and whose unconventional technique has ushered in a conspicuous change in the arena of modern literature.

As Seth is both poet and prose-writer, the chief strength of his style is that he is able to artistically blend the poet's sensitivity with the narrator's comprehension of the elements of plot, structure, and character. In this respect, Seth is unique. I became extremely impressed with Seth's writings after reading his works, in particular his poetry and his verse novel *The Golden Gate*. Seth's works reveal an attempt to go back to earlier models of literary tradition without compromising his modernity. Through his writing, Seth has endeavoured to keep alive in modern literature all the salient features of the literature of yore. Thus, he goes back to Byron, to Pushkin, to Tolstoy, to nineteenth century England, to T'ang dynasty of China, to Chaucer, to the Elizabethans, the Romantics, to name but a few—in essence, to some of the greatest names in the literature of the world.

With his appropriation of literary traditions from all corners of the globe, Seth has taken modern Indian English writing beyond the ken of national boundaries. Seth has been able to transcend the magnetic pull of India to emerge into the bigger orbit of the world. This enables him to write global literature, not just Indian English literature. Yet, Seth's achievements are more than boundary-crossing as represented in dining on multi-ethnic cuisine; he has truly apprehended what it means to be a citizen of the world, even as he holds on to his Indian roots. His aim has been to assimilate the best in world culture and then to incorporate it into his writing. This effort has been more or less a subconscious one, shaped by Seth's eclectic reading, his peripatetic lifestyle, and by his receptivity to different influences.

Seth has achieved enviable international renown, but I was distressed to note that no profound or penetrating work exploring the entire range of his literary output has yet been undertaken on his protean genius—a genius that can apply itself to all kinds of literary genres. I realized that the weight and substance of Seth's works have not been properly studied, and his contribution to world literature has not been suitably evaluated. Both these factors prompted me to undertake this study.

In this book an attempt has been made to chart the development of Vikram Seth's art, tracing in a chronological context its growth and correlating it with his personal life—following the various phases of his experiences, the stages of his mental and emotional maturity, and the subsequent changes undergone by his art.

I hope that scholars studying writings in Indian English will find this book helpful, and any suggestions, for its improvement in the next edition are welcome.

I would like to take this opportunity to express my gratitude to my prestigious publishers, Atlantic Publishers and Distributors, for taking interest in this work. I express my gratitude to my mentor, Prof. Sushma Sharma, for her invaluable suggestions. I also acknowledge the cooperation of Jahnavi and Divija for being loving in the way only daughters can be, and to my husband, Aashish, for his unfailing love and support.

ROOPALI GUPTA

Contents

Contents

1

The Artist and His Grounding

The name Vikram Seth conjures up the image of an erudite cosmopolite, one who has baffled critics and readers alike as a writer who has epic, yet unpredictable talents. He seems to be able to juggle words with consummate ease, and his pen wields both poetry and prose with equal dexterity. He has made the English language his own, unselfconsciously authoring works as diverse as his slim volumes of poetry to the leviathan sized *A Suitable Boy*, and with his trademark transparent style, he has gone a long way towards reinventing the contemporary literary scene.

Born on June 20, 1952, to Justice Leila Seth and Mr. Prem Seth (a shoe company executive), Vikram Seth is the oldest of three children. Seth received his primary school education in Dehradun, at the prestigious Doon School, the alumni list of which boasts many of India's rich and famous personalities. This elitist boarding school education equipped Seth with the confidence and the linguistic tools to fit in abroad and it also cultivated in him a predilection for the literary culture of England (as being part of the school curriculum). In an interview with Pavan K. Verma, Seth says, "We are all accidents of history. We must accept that. If you have been taught to play the sarangi, you cannot suddenly switch to sitar. So, perhaps, I must accept that English is my lot."[1] This literary anglophilism inspired by Seth's schooling during his formative years is the cornerstone of Seth's literary culture.

Seth's genius was evident right from his Doon School days. A 1965 school report, when he was 13, calls him "super excellent, he is a giant in versatility."[2] Those were prophetic words. From Doon School, Seth won a scholarship to the Tonbridge School, Kent, England, from where he won another scholarship, to Oxford. He took his undergraduate degree in PPE (philosophy, politics, and economics) from Corpus Christi College, Oxford (B.A. 1975).

It was at Oxford that Seth, unhappily in love as a university student, began to write poetry. Seth condemns these early poems, saying that back then he was "incredibly unskilful."[3] However, he continued to write, keeping these poems to himself and writing them primarily for his own pleasure. Then for his post-graduate degree, Seth left for Stanford University, California, U.S.A. It was at Stanford that being an avid reader of poetry as well, he stumbled upon the translated works of T'ang dynasty Chinese poet Wang Wei. Seth was so affected by these poems that he decided to learn Mandarin so that he could read the Chinese masters in the original, and demonstrated his intellectual brilliance by learning the language so quickly that he was writing poetry in Mandarin within a year. By now, he had also started writing poetry in English more seriously. Aware that he needed guidance, Seth approached the teachers of the English department at Stanford, and found a mentor in poet Timothy Steele, who then held a Jones Lectureship in poetry at Stanford. It was Steele who provided the sustaining support for this brilliant undergraduate with a flair for writing and an urge for creativity. Timothy Steele recounts:

> The first thing that impresses you about Vikram is his immense and lively intelligence. It was always clear he was going to do something remarkable, but it wasn't clear, when I first knew him, what direction his talent would take. Three or four muses were tugging jealously at him [...].[4]

Timothy Steele agreed to give Seth an informal biweekly tutorial, and in this manner the would-be economist took a year's leave from the economics department for a Wallace

Stegner fellowship in creative writing (1977-78). Seth was also considerably influenced by Donald Davie—the English poet and critic—also at Stanford at the time, and he was a contemporary of Dana Gioia (also at Stanford), who's *Can Poetry Matter?*[5] heralded the doom of the confessional, anything-goes poetry that was being churned out of American Universities.

Both Steele and Davie are fine, formal poets, and under their joint influence, Seth's natural inclination to write in rhyme and meter bore fruit. His first collection of poems, *Mappings*, came out in 1980, after he had rejoined the economics department.

Mappings is introspective, as poets' first collections often are. In it he explores all the themes that recur in his later poetry: love, friendship, loneliness, loss, expatriation, nature, and social conscientiousness—all from his trademark mock-humorous stance.

Most of the poems in this first collection were in rhyme and meter and consequently quite unfashionable. Rejected by every publisher he tried, Seth typeset, published, and distributed the book himself, pedalling it around the Bay area bookstores, forcing copies on to family and friends, exhorting them to sell them if they could and to give them away if they couldn't.[6] *Mappings* was later published by the Writers' Workshop in Calcutta. By then, Seth had left for China's Nanjing University, for his doctoral research in economics on the demography of Chinese villages. In China, Seth spent less time on his research and more on reading poems in Chinese [a pastime that ultimately resulted in *Three Chinese Poets—the translated poems of Wang Wei, Du Fu, and Li Bai* (1992)]. It was towards the end of his stay in China, during an organized sight-seeing trip to China's north-west province that Seth managed to charm a Chinese policeman with his rendition of "main awara hoon," from the Hindi blockbuster movie "Awara," which was very popular in China at the time. The next day his singing was the talk of the local police station, and after a lengthy debate on the merits of Indian film stars, Seth managed to wangle a rarely given permit to travel to

Lhasa, the Tibetan capital in China's forbidden land, and decided to hitchhike his way back home to India via Tibet.[7] This intriguing journey was published in 1983 by London publishers Chatto and Windus as the travelogue *From Heaven Lake*. The success of this travelogue was greatly responsible for giving Seth the confidence to think of himself as a writer.

Back at Stanford in 1983, Seth was busy in analyzing the results of the demographic survey he had done in China when he was interrupted by the literary muse again. The result was a collection of poems called *The Humble Administrator's Garden*, published in 1985. This volume was the culmination of Seth's varied cultural experiences: Indian, Chinese, and Californian. During these years (1983-85), Seth read another book that was to change the course of his life: Alexander Pushkin's *Eugene Onegin*.[8] Looking for a break from his humdrum economic data-crunching, Seth visited a bookstore and chanced upon a dog-eared copy of *Eugene Onegin* in a Charles Johnston translation. Seth recounts, "After reading that, it obsessed me. I couldn't think of writing anything else—certainly not my dissertation."[9] So it was that *The Golden Gate* was written, and published in 1986 by Random House. This verse-novel won Seth the *Commonwealth Poetry Prize* in 1986, and catapulted him into the limelight. Apart from its obvious literary merits, the book was a landmark in Seth's career for it gave Seth a stepping stone into the realm of fiction from an area in which he felt confident, namely poetry. *The Golden Gate* adroitly traverses this bridge between poetry and prose, and as Seth says, "I didn't know I was a novelist until I wrote The Golden Gate."[10]

The Golden Gate is an in-depth exploration of society, specifically American society. With a surgeon's precision Seth examines the fabric of contemporary American society, and pinpoints the factors that are tearing it apart. Critics deride the novel for being hedonistic but on a closer scrutiny it becomes clear that not only does the novel argue against a hedonistic lifestyle, it also manages to make good sense of the chaos that permeates every stratum of a fast paced culture, even suggesting remedial measures.

Given *The Golden Gate's* reception, it was perhaps inevitable that Seth abandoned his Ph.D. in economics and became a full time writer. Returning to his parents' house in Delhi in 1987, Seth began work on *A Suitable Boy*. In the six years it took to write the novel, Seth won another award—the Central Sahitya Academy award (1988) for *The Golden Gate*, and published three more volumes of poetry: *All You Who Sleep Tonight* (1990), *Beastly Tales from Here And There* (1991), and *Three Chinese Poets* (1993).

As with Seth's earlier collections of poetry [*Mappings*, and *The Humble Administrator's Garden]*, *All You Who Sleep Tonight* is intensely personal, in which Seth resolves issues about love, friendship, familial ties, the loneliness of living in a foreign land and so on. Many of Seth's recurring themes of nostalgia, detachment, observation and exile coalesce here. These are the things that troubled Seth at that stage in his life, and in these poems he voices most of these thoughts, dealing with issues that henceforth do not reappear in his poetry. Writing these poems was thus a kind of catharsis that enabled Seth to come to terms with the vicissitudes of his life.

Beastly Tales is a delightful collection of fables retold in verse with Seth's inimitable charm. The light hearted spirit in which it is written speaks volumes for Seth's state of mind at the time he wrote these tales, a time when he is languishing in the heat of a merciless summer afternoon, while it is too hot to concentrate on the more substantial *A Suitable Boy*. Being a retelling of fables, the themes are essentially social and humanitarian, but Seth gives them a subtle twist here and there to make the stories co-temporal in their relevance to the ironies of life. In this work, as in *The Golden Gate*, Seth pauses to reflect on the changed values of mankind, portraying the effect these new values have upon one's life. The book is written with verbal levity, but its themes run deep and serious.

Three Chinese Poets is the final product of Seth's stay in China. Though this work is strictly for avid fans of poetry, it is worthwhile to note here how this collection highlights two things—namely, Seth's interest in literature and how it takes shape, and secondly his conscientiousness as an artist, as evinced by the foreword to this collection, in which he presents a brief history of T'ang dynasty China in order to put the three translated poets into perspective.

Following these books, London publishers Orion published Seth's *A Suitable Boy* in 1994, and Seth created literary history with the book's mammoth size and the million copies sales. *A Suitable Boy* was conceived by a very Jane Austen-ish shred of overheard conversation: "You too will marry a boy I choose [...]." For Seth this theme proved to be irresistible and he set out to write a story involving a widow's search for a 'suitable' (in the Indian context) bridegroom for her daughter. Seth intended it to be a short piece, written with a rekindling of Jane Austen's sublime subtlety of humour. *A Suitable Boy* was thus meant to be a social novel, in the tradition of the realistic social novels of the nineteenth century, although Seth had not intended it to be quite so long. The novel is in effect a throwback to an earlier generation of writers. With regard to this novel it is noteworthy that although the subject matter of the book is India of the 1950s, *A Suitable Boy* is not an 'Indian' novel in the sense that Seth does not try to force his ethnicity on the reader. His stance is that of the keen and tolerant observer attempting to re-create a story about life, life that is full of unexpected events, sometimes sad, but for the most part, comic.

Like *The Golden Gate*, *A Suitable Boy* also proved to be another landmark in Seth's career on account of the novel's unprecedented success. In its aftermath, Seth found himself in the literary stratosphere. But with the accolades went a lot of hard work: interviews, book tours, readings, and so on—all taking their toll on a writer's most valuable commodity: solitude. Seth says that it took him six years to write *A Suitable Boy* and adds that "it took me another three to recover from it,"[11] and it becomes evident that he is only half-joking. By then Seth had started living, for the most part, in London and in 1994, he was commissioned by the Baylis National Opera to write *Arion And The Dolphin* (1994), based on the classical story of the musician Arion.

Inspiration once again struck, in the year 1997-98, and the muse this time was music. In 1999 Seth published *An Equal Music*, an extraordinary novel about music and love, culled from his experience of chamber-music in England. Seth's love for music started early, when in his childhood he learned to play the flute and trained to sing. But his introduction to western classical music came late, when he was taken by a friend to hear Bach while he was at Oxford. This first induction into western classical music began a life long passion, one that was to finally culminate in *An Equal Music*.

An Equal Music marks a breaking away from Seth's earlier self-controlled and distanced style of writing. The reason for this becomes clear when Seth reveals how for him music acts as a refuge from the tensions of work, how he found it difficult to reconcile himself to the thought of writing about it.[12] Music amounts to a passion, almost an obsession with Seth, and this is evident from the style in which *An Equal Music* has been written—so different from Seth's previous work, as he strives to capture the essence of music in words.

The contrast is sheer also because this is a novel written in the first person, unlike Seth's earlier third person narrative. The book is therefore less under Seth's control—the characters assume more importance as Seth is forced to give them a certain amount of leeway. The emphasis is on the theme rather than on the story, unlike in *The Golden Gate* and *A Suitable Boy*, and Seth's erstwhile levity is lost somewhere on the way. It is more than coincidence that there is a certain darkness in *An Equal Music*; it has a melancholic strain running through it that mirrors a corresponding sadness in Seth's mind. Seth admits this and says that "I drew upon my own experiences of having been in emotional states like Michael's."[13] *An Equal Music* is thus a departure from Seth's earlier work; it represents a sort of coming-of–age, as Seth replaces the part ironic, part-humorous treatment he usually accords to love with an intensity, almost a compulsion, to explore its more serious side. There is no doubt that Seth has a balanced head on his shoulders when it comes to love—as evinced from his earlier work—where he seems to be telling the reader to take love at its face value, not to imbue it with more importance than it deserves. But in *An Equal Music*, Seth's love for music sweeps all reservations aside, as he discovers and articulates what it means to be so passionately in love, whether with a person or with an art form.

These ten works currently make up Seth's oeuvre, and from the above it becomes evident that a peripatetic lifestyle has moulded the themes and shapes of most of his work. As Seth says, "I've been quartered between California, China, India, and England."[14] An apt analogy, but Seth's interest in these four cultures is not that of the detached observer content merely to portray the exotic—it is rather that of the studious, interested learner bent on apprehending the essence of them all. C. Vijaysree points out that "His (Seth's) work reveals the response of an expansive Indian sensibility to the richness of varied cultures outside: he does not resist influences, reject the possibilities of alternate points of view, or disapprove of divergences."[15]

It will be worthwhile to note here that Seth takes time out to absorb a foreign culture before venturing to write about it and consequently, his work always bears the stamp of authenticity, no matter how alien the locale. Even in the case of a novel as Indian in theme as *A Suitable Boy*, Seth did not take on the subcontinent before he was good and ready, aware that just the fact that he was an Indian did not make him intrinsically qualified to write about India.

Apart from Seth's travels, his eclectic reading has also had tremendous impact on his own literary tastes and beliefs, and consequently, on his art. And as befitting an author who freely acknowledges his literary influences, allusion is at the heart of Seth's style, and behind this allusion is a wealth of earlier literature—Chaucer, the Elizabethans, the Romantics, the poetry of Hardy, T'ang dynasty Chinese poets and so on, which makes it fairly easy to assess Seth's work on the basis of literary recapitulation. Seth says about his literary preferences:

> The kind of books I like reading are books where the authorial voice doesn't intrude too much—nineteenth

> century novels, and some twentieth century novels as well. They don't try to pull you up with the brilliance of their sentences as much as pull you into a world.[16]

These would be novelists like Jane Austen, George Eliot, and closer home, the doyen of Indian English fiction, R.K. Narayan, whom Seth by self-confession, cannot resist reading.

Seth's subject matter is almost invariably love, in all its myriad manifestations. He does explore other themes in passing —India's political landscape for instance, or religious frenzy, but in these instances his role is always that of storyteller, not of commentator. He does feel strongly about issues like religious intolerance, nuclear non-proliferation, but he is not a social activist. Consequently, there is no social gravitas in his writing. He feels that "the characters should ring true to the peoples' lives they portray. Political thoughts should come naturally to characters, they should not be a trampoline for my political thoughts."[17] Seth's characters are thus chiefly involved in getting on with their lives, and as an artist Seth's primary concern is to portray them indulging in activities that are, in a general sense, common to all humanity. Seth also places great emphasis on the redeeming aspects of private life, portraying in his work that happiness and tolerance start from the home. The unifying theme that runs through his work is the plea for human camaraderie, spanning political, national, and cultural barriers. Seth's writing is an embodiment of his intrinsic tolerance, a tolerance that is remarkably Chaucer-like, extending itself to include all the foibles of human behaviour, and evident specially in his acute distress at the destruction of humanity by humans.

Seth is firm about his priorities as an artist. He places clarity and intelligibility above verbal pyrotechnics. Also, he tends towards realism in all his work. He says, "I tend to write realistic novels [...]. I would feel that I've failed the characters in my book if I didn't describe their world reasonably accurately."[18] This is evident in Seth's re-creation of worlds which always ring true, whether he is writing a story about west-coast America, India of the 1950s, or the world of

Schubert and Mozart. However, Seth believes like Goethe that the artist's work is real in so far as it is always true; ideal in that it is never actual. Seth is an accomplished artist and treads with considerable poise this fine line, rendering the near and the familiar with artistic verisimilitude.

But the pièce de résistance of Seth's style is his inimitable blending of what constitutes the common man's bread with literary manna. In a similar vein to the eighteenth century gentlemen Addison and Steele, Seth's endeavour has been to free the contemporary novel of its seriousness, its high-brow contempt for the simple passions, its increasingly academic concerns with critics and deconstructionists—in which that unimportant entity, the ordinary reader, is all but forgotten—in order to make literature un-daunting and accessible for the general reader. For Seth, writing is a simple business that has been diverted from its original course by an over-emphasis on style and modernist knowingness. Seth says:

> I don't read a lot of modern fiction, but it seems to me that too much of it is thesis fodder. Since the rise of the academic critic, writing has had to have an increased sophistication, as if subjects such as love, ambition, and family are worthy only of the airport novel. Writers come out of university courses and carry into their writing academic concerns rather than the concerns of the general reader.[19]

Seth's awareness of this trend and his conscious shunning of it are what make his work so approachable. He does not try to constantly force the reader to appreciate his command over language, and his approach to fiction is unselfconsciously anti-modernist. His literary mammoth, *A Suitable Boy*, even at 1300+ pages, is so accessible to the general reader that even when it ends, the reader has not had enough and wants to know what happens next. Similarly, *An Equal Music*, despite being substantially technical, far from putting off the musically uneducated, carries the reader along in a general sense, so that one seems to hear the music that one never knew. Even Seth's poetry is not of the kind that is difficult to read and even more difficult to interpret, for he places great emphasis on clarity and on the directness of utterance.

Much has been made of Seth's experimentation with different genres—but Seth writes as and how the muse takes him, and the different genres are a spontaneous unfolding of his protean talent rather than lucubrated attempts at diversity. Seth has been unjustly accused of not having found his voice, and he counters with "the fact is that at different stages of your life and under the influence of different inspirations, you write different things."[20]

Seth also points out, rather astutely, that "If you're tapped on the shoulder and inspired to do something, you don't say, 'my training isn't in this.' I just let the imagination work."[21]

He further says, in his precise, poetic way:

> The wish to write about is such a rare and mysterious feeling that it is pointless to pre-empt or constrain it by notions of subject or geography or genre [...]. For good or ill, one must take one's visions as they come and be thankful for those that survive.[22]

There is no doubt that with his technique, both inherited and innovative, and his refreshing attitude towards the creative process Seth has transformed the literary arena and dazzled both the East and the West as a writer with profound promise. The diversity and range of Seth's work makes him somewhat of an enigma. However, for a writer who counts such diverse figures as Pushkin, T'ang dynasty Chinese poets, Chaucer, the Elizabethans, Tennyson, novelists like Hardy, Austen, George Eliot, R.K. Narayan, and modern poets like Timothy Steele and Philip Larkin among some of his literary influences, Seth's wide-ranging technique is conceivably not so surprising. Perhaps, like of Goethe, it can be said of Seth that he has no style, only styles. But whatever be the externals of his technique, there can no doubt that with writing, this economics post-graduate has finally found his métier.

Notes

1. Pavan K. Verma, "Of Love, Loneliness and the Fine Art of Storytelling," *Hindustan Times* (Delhi), *Sunday Magazine*, May 2, 1999.

2. Jeremy Gavron, "A Suitable Joy," *Daily Mail* and *Guardian*, July 20, 1999.
3. *Ibid.*
4. Cynthia Haven, "Poetic Licence," *Stanford Magazine* (May/June 1999).
5. Dana Gioia, "Can Poetry Matter?" *The Atlantic Monthly*; May, 1991; Volume 267, No. 5; 94-106.
6. "Introduction to the 1994 edition," *Mappings*, Viking Penguin India, 1994, ix.
7. From *Heaven Lake*, 11-14.
8. Pushkin, *Eugene Onegin*.
9. Haven, *loc cit*.
10. Vikram Seth, "Writers on Writing," *Radio Series Transcript*, Australian Broadcasting Corporation. URL:http://www.abc.net.au/writers/writesummary.htm
11. Rediff.com Interview URL:www.rediff.com/chat/vikcha.htm
12. Author's note, *An Equal Music*, Viking Books, 1999.
13. Akash Kapur, "The Seth Variations," *Atlantic Unbound Interview*. URL:www.theatlantic.com/unbound/interviews/ba990623.htm
14. Sharon Verghis, "Symphony of words from the man who found a Beethoven Opus," the *Sydney Morning Herald*, March 13, 2000.
15. C. Vijaysree, "Vikram Seth," *Writers of the India Diaspora*, ed. Emmanuel S. Nelson, Greenwood Press, CT, © 1993.
16. Amit V. Raghavan, Interview, Spring 1999. URL: www.emory.edu/ENGLISH/Bahri/Seth.html
17. Chandra Chakrabarti, "Seth—Suitably both a Writer and a Citizen," *Indian Reporter* (Illinois), USA.
18. Writers on writing, *loc cit*.
19. Gavron, *loc cit*.
20. Kapur, *loc cit*.
21. Geeta Sharma-Jensen, "Poetry or Prose, East or West, Seth simply follows his muse," *Milwaukee Journal Sentinel*, May 21, 2000.
22. "Introduction," *The Poems* 1981-1994, Penguin India, 1995, xv.

2

The Conflict between Predilection and Medium

It is a truism that poetry is seldom read and even more seldom appreciated. It is certainly accorded less attention, even by reviewers and critics, than fiction. Vikram Seth knows this and says, "Poetry lists the preserves of people who do not expect to sell."[1]

But Seth, by predilection, is primarily a poet, and not withstanding concern about sales, he thinks of himself as a poet rather than as a novelist. The conflict arises because ironically enough, it is his novels that have brought him greater renown.

The fact that Seth began to write novels at the same time that he continued to write poetry is not surprising. This is because though Seth began his foray into literature as a poet, he was not one to disappoint the muse when she knocked on his door, and was willing to try his hand at anything, once inspiration had struck. Thus, his first collection of poems (*Mappings*) was followed by the award-winning prose travelogue *From Heaven Lake*. This was followed by *The Humble Administrator's garden*, another collection of poems. Then Seth wrote his verse novel, *The Golden Gate*, followed by three more volumes of poetry: *All You Who Sleep Tonight*, *Three Chinese Poets*, and *Beastly Tales from Here And There*. These were followed by *A Suitable Boy*, then the opera text *Arion and the Dolphin*, and finally, *An Equal Music*.

From a perusal of the above it becomes clear that although Seth has tried his hand at several types of writing, poetry is the form that is predominant. Even his prose, as evinced in *From Heaven Lake*, and *An Equal Music*, is more poetical than prose-like, and *A Suitable Boy* contains a fair amount of versification. Poetry comes more or less naturally to Seth and there is no gainsaying that his sensibility is essentially poetic.

As mentioned earlier, Seth began to write poetry in his university days; most of these poems were in free verse, but Seth gradually found himself writing in a more orderly form. The reason for this shift is expatiated upon by Seth:

> I have read a great deal of the free verse of other poets, some of it—such as the poems of Whitman or Lawrence—with a great deal of pleasure. But the lines that come to my mind when I need poetry—to delight or remind or suggest or console—are almost invariably in meter, and often in rhyme [...]. Since verse "in form" is what I usually find myself reading, it is what I almost always find myself writing.[2]

Belonging as he does to the present age of vers libre, Seth had thus inadvertently become an iconoclast. He describes his dilemma, saying that since he was studying economics, not English, he stood outside the orbit of the latest critical theories and did not realize that writing in rhyme and meter would make him a sort of literary untouchable.[3]

As he faced rejection, Seth felt apprehensive that writing in traditional meters would mark him as a "fuddy-duddy," but his doubts were laid to rest after exposure to Timothy Steele's poetry and the work of Frost and Larkin. Seth says, "I learned that you could write in form and still be very much of your time, using patterns that had been used for centuries."[4]

Seth thus unselfconsciously recognizes and admires his literary predecessors, but his fidelity to his chosen medium is not in the nature of slavish imitation or even postmodernist pastiche. Like all true artists, he appropriates literary tradition and moulds it around his own sensibility, creating in the process poetry that goes back for its form to the ordered rhythm and metre of the poetry of yore but has very contemporaneous subject matter.

Drawing naturally as Seth does on an international milieu, his poetic output is authenticated in its awareness of more than one tradition. Seth himself is not interested in literary theory. He calls the deconstructionists and other Littcrit types "the mad critics."[5] However, he is part of a contemporary trend among poets towards Formalism.

Like Keats, Seth seems to believe that if poetry does not come spontaneously then it had better not come at all. The best among the Indo-Anglian poets seem to agree with Wallace Stevens when he says, "poetry has to be more than a conception of the mind. It has to be a revelation of nature. Conceptions are artificial, perceptions are essential."[6] It is perceptions that one discerns in Nissim Ezekiel's poems, in Kamala Das, and in Seth. In effect, Seth seems to appropriate the Imagist gains of the first phase of modern English poetry.

Seth writes poetry in which memory plays a vigorous, creative role. He summons from the hinterland of memory moments of emotional association and expresses them as poems. This re-creation of the past in living memory is the equivalent of an emotional release in the form of a poem. The expression is characterised by its evocation of concrete images, crystal-clear lines of thought, and a serene, equable emotion—by means of which an emotional equilibrium is achieved. The poems are personal poems, revealing the poet's preoccupations and his personality. In addition, Seth's poetic technique involves the use of directness of utterance. The tendency to find an objective co-relative for his feelings, like Eliot, is not in Seth's repertoire. The strength of his style is that it is lucid without being simplistic, emotional without being cloying.

The three volumes of poetry discussed in this chapter: *Mappings*, *The Humble Administrator's Garden*, and *All You Who Sleep Tonight*, have a common thread running through them: they are all intensely personal and subjective, and consequently, autobiographical to a great extent. In addition, these poems are deeply introspective, and in them appears the only hint of an expatriate sensibility that Seth reveals in his work.

I. MAPPINGS

Mappings, Seth first collection of poetry, which he disparagingly terms as his "juvenilia,"[7] though not really representative of Seth's poetic oeuvre, nevertheless contains the only poems influenced by his stay in England that he has published. In this first collection, "adherence to his chosen forms almost forces itself upon one's notice."[8]

Seth's poetic temperament, in conjunction with his poetic sensibility, is in evidence even in this maiden work. The predominant mood in which these poems were written is one discoloured by disappointment in love, but the poems are remarkable for the courage they reveal, inherent in the acceptance of life as it is, and the effort to go on with it in spite of setbacks and heartbreak.

The poems in *Mappings* can be collated into thematic groups. One such group comprises of poems dealing with familial ties and issues about expatriation. These poems all reveal Seth's strong feelings for his family and his acute perception about his own break from his roots. There is a little sadness, a little wonder, but above all there is acceptance, both of physical and emotional distancing.

In *Panipat*, Seth is home during a break from his studies in London, but he feels alienated from his surroundings. The song of the koyal does not draw him back into his childhood but calls to mind other English birds whose song he has grown to love, and English trees under whose shade he has spent leisure hours. It is finally the taste of a mango that forces upon his senses that "I must be home at last" (2).

Departure-Lounge is a delicate exploration of a fragile and uneasy father-son relationship. There is the knowledge that precious years have been lost and that both time and distances have left them too alienated to bond, but there is also the warm, gentle joy that comes from knowing that there is love shared as well.

Rakhi reveals Seth's tender feelings for his sister and is remarkable because it adroitly expresses a world of meaning with an economy of words.

Home Thoughts from the Bay leaves Seth likening himself to a day moon loitering absently in the sky, and expresses all the doubts that come in the wake of expatriation.

Divali is a longer poem that intricately explores the expatriate sensibility. The delineation is such that the poem ceases to be merely subjective and broadens into a coming-to-terms with expatriate reality that most expatriates can probably identify with. The poet feels keenly the dread of being in a foreign land. His school life has equipped him with the keys not only to a job, power, and the good life, but also to a nowhere land where the legacy he has inherited is snobbery, a kind of group narcissism, and an impalpable fear. Seth accurately reveals the Indian elite's mentality towards the West: aping Western customs, fawning over foreigners, considering themselves to be a superior breed of Indians, even as they are humiliatingly sidelined in the West:

[...] I know that the whole world
Means exile for our breed
Who are not at home at home
And are abroad abroad [...] (67).

The poem however deals successfully with all these issues and concludes on a note of acceptance. Seth is content not to expect that life will give him everything; the beauty of Nature, the languid notes of a flute, the still beauty of architecture—all lull him into a world where he is no longer an exile, even if the solace in only fleeting. He finally decides, "But freedom? The notes would sing [...]/Parole is enough" (69).

Some of the poems deal with love fulfilled. These are all bathed in the warm glow of love found and are effervescent like champagne; they bubble with sheer happiness and the reader feels that Seth's cup truly runneth over with measureless contentment. Seth serenades his love like a medieval lover, and almost burns incense at her feet. These poems are also remarkable for their humour—whether Seth is describing a chance encounter in the course of a long flight or a lazy Sunday morning spent in bed. Poems like *Aubade* and *Sonnet* speak eloquently about the nature of Seth's love, showing how he is totally caught up in the moment. *The Sultan's Turret* is one of the funniest poems of the lot. Two poems, *Guest*, and *Dubious*, are unique in that they portray homosexuality. These poems are brave ones, both for the relative ease with which Seth speaks of the subject, and for the total disregard he feels for the censure of the world.

Seth speaks of love lost with a remarkable poignancy. Anyone who has ever loved and lost will recognize in these meditative poems the soulful mourning of the passing of love. *To Manijeh*, *The Walkers*, *At Evening* are some of the poems in this group. Seth is clearly a sensitive soul, very much in touch with all his feelings. Love is central to his existence, making him soar with the eagles when he has it in his grasp, and plunging him into the bottomless, inky depths of despair when it eludes him. But he is resilient enough to survive. So he says, in *The Balcony*:

> If I have bent so far and not snapped, it
> Cannot destroy me now. This thing will pass
> As it has passed before. Elation is
> No birthright [...] (38).

Distressful Homonyms also deals with love lost and its acceptance. Seth reaches the conclusion that "[...] love, like the rest/of our emotions, sometimes needs a rest" (57). *Progress Report* has been written in a slightly sardonic vein, attempting to disguise the pain felt at parting. *Quaking Bridge* also belongs in this section.

Seth's nature poems are of two types—one type is purely objective, describing Nature *per se*, the other is subjective, in which the poet deals with his pain by hoping that Mother Nature will wrap a numbing blanket around him. *A Winter Word* belongs to the latter, while *Grand Canyon* is a marvellous example of the former, capturing the quintessence of California's great landmark in four short lines. *Tomatoes* is again subjective, conjuring up scenes of Nature in relation to the poet and his world. *Rain* pulsates with a feeling of quiet desperation, a hope for even a temporary reprieve from the cares of the world, and is moving in its simplicity. *After Three Years* finds the poet seeking the meaning of existence in the resiliency of Nature in surviving the worst of blights, and drawing hope and inspiration from it.

From Mount Tamalpais exhibits Seth's knack for describing the phenomena of Nature with a unique blending of the facts of science with the imaginative faculty. Describing the flight of eagles he says:

[...] Their effort lies
In sensed surrender
To the heat's rise
From the earth under

In which suspense
Their cruise would appear
Less hunt than dance
With shadow and air [...] (30).

Moths and *Point Reyes* are pure Nature descriptions. The wit and brevity incorporated into both these poems is strongly reminiscent of the charged poetry of Emily Dickinson. *Moonless Night* is a seeking of parallels for the human predicament in the workings of Nature.

A group of poems are *Bagatelles* and *Six Octets*. Here Seth is in his jocular mood. Some of the octets in *Six Octets* speak of love lost but mostly they display humour and wit, and also the poet's good sense in being able to laugh at himself and in not taking himself too seriously.

Some poems meditate on the complexities of life. These are poems like *Switching Off* and *Mappings*—poetry that is born of pain, forced from the soul by suffering. *Switching off* objectifies the fear of death, *Even Such* attempts to deal with grief, *Close of Play* portrays brilliantly mankind's collective headlong rush towards certain doom, being brought about by nuclear madness:

[...] Too late we perceive
Our playthings, grown autonomous, knowledge and use,
This practical, that ideal Good at last
Rear doom toys that will undo nine-tenths of us
Leaving the breathing dead we call survivors
On a radiant waste [...] (41).

The poem powerfully expresses sentiments that any sane person will doubtless share; it shows that life can be good, but notes with despair that if man's blindness continues unabated, the earth will soon be blasted off into lifelessness, like the rest of the planets in the solar system. Seth says in the end, "It is a pity/But nothing new to an old universe" (42).

Mappings (the poem), characterises the tone of the entire collection. The keynote of the poem is the acceptance of life as an evolutionary process, in the course of which one leaves in one's wake experiences and memories that mould one's character. The basic tenet is that one does not change completely over the years—one evolves, and every facet of one's erstwhile self is hidden just beneath the surface, blending with what one is now and forming a composite whole. The sharp visual images conjure up the scene:

[...] That was a younger self. I want to touch
His shoulder, make him smile, show him how each
Sorrow or failure that lacerates his heart
Can heal or numb itself [...] (61).

The poem is a valuable exercise in learning how to live with oneself. One may not like or approve of any one part, but nevertheless, it must be accepted and accounted for. *A Morning Walk* finds Seth in a socially conscientious frame of mind. The poem, apart from betraying the pain of expatriation, is an extremely heartfelt piece, prompted by the misery in which the people of India live. Seth says, "To wander through the streets of Calcutta is/To force the whole world's misery on the heart" (71). The poet is guilt ridden that, "Food, shelter, health, are mine; interests; loves;/The time to walk through avocado groves" (71), while in India people die daily for want of the price of tea and a slice. Seth says further:

[...] I draw my non-consumptive breath,
Think life sweet, spin rhymes, eat my daily fly
And neither shrink before nor welcome death
But others, even those who fear to die,
Suffer with quietude, with spent relief,
The final amnesty from want and grief (72).

The parallels have been drawn not for the sake of feeling good about his own life—they stem from a feeling of helplessness at the unbridgability of the abyss between the haves and the have-nots, the difference of affluence between America and India. The poem reveals Seth's innate compassion.

There are also a few translations: one from the Chinese of Du Fu, one from the Urdu of Faiz Ahmed Faiz, one from the German of Heinrich Heinz, and from the Hindi of Suryakant Tripathi Nirala.

Mappings is thus chiefly a collection of personal poems that speak of love, alienation, and borders on a brooding self-analysis. The title is appropriate, quite in keeping with the basic theme of the poems, which dwell in the past and chart out the poet's course in his early university years. There is in these poems a candidness that addresses itself to the heart and touches the soul in the way all great poetry does. Many of these poems furnish the bits and pieces about Seth's life; others reveal a maturity of the thought process that is startling in one so young. These early poems have unmistakable emotion behind them, and its expression is such that it invites the reader to share in the poet's joy or pain. This is what constitutes the charm of this first collection.

II. THE HUMBLE ADMINISTRATOR'S GARDEN

This collection is a travelogue of sorts. It is primarily visual and reflective, merging nostalgia with a traveller's sense of detachment and observation. Nature is omnipresent, even the sections into which the book is divided taking their names from an arboreal theme. The poet reflects on three cultures that he has known—Chinese, Indian, and Californian, and each culture is represented by a tree that is the symbolic embodiment of its respective geographical location: the

Wu-Tong tree for China, Neem for India, and Live-Oak for California.

The trifurcation is noteworthy not only for its cultural connotations but also for the way in which it reflects the poet's state of mind in each of these places. While writing about China, Seth is moved primarily by the landscape and the people—he finds the Zen gardens and the simplicity of the people fascinating. In the Neem section he is at home and consequently chiefly autobiographical, and in Live-Oak he grapples with issues about expatriation, love, a fast-paced culture.

In the 'Wu-Tong' section of poems about China, Seth is at peace with himself and with the world, and "the poet's eye is on what is objectively before him, rather than on the intricacies of his own sensibility."[9] Some of these poems are picturesque landscape descriptions. Seth's art employs such graphic images that the poems are like snapshots of moments frozen in time. Such poems include *The Master-of-Nets Garden*, *The Humble Administrator's garden*, *The Gentle Waves Pavilion*, *The Tarrying Garden*, *Evening Wheat*, *A Hanhzhou Garden*. None of these poems is longer than fourteen lines, but the words come to life and turn into pictures. Seth uses a clever juxtaposition of the senses: colour, smell, touch, the play of light and shadow, to achieve this effect. Seth's portrayal of Nature has a kinship with the Pre-Raphaelites, with their emphasis on the photographic replication of a scene in words. Seth achieves this effect without being archaic and yet without compromising quality. The effect that is produced by employing the simplest of words is astonishing. To illustrate:

THE MASTER-OF-NETS GARDEN

Magnolia petals fall, pale, fragrant, brown
Resting on moss within a square of white;
Courtyard of quietness, of intimate stone
And Latticed Shadow. Outside, low at night,
Three moons—of water, mirror, sky—define
Pine and old Cypress struggling against the stars,
And jasmine and gardenia combine
Their scent with that of closed magnolias (40).

Apart from these scenic portrayals, the other poems in the Wu-Tong section depict life in Chinese cities. In China, Seth does not feel like a foreigner, like he does in London or California. This is not surprising, considering the many similarities between India and China, and the disparities between India and the West. *A Little Night Music*, *The North Temple Tower*, *Nanjing Night*, *The Accountant's House*, *Research in Jiangsu Province*, *From an 'East is Red' Steamer* are such. *The great Confucian Temple, Suzhou*, is a purely descriptive poem, while *The North Temple Tower* is subtly humorous. *Nanjing Night* captures the essence of life in a big Chinese city, with its characteristic sounds and sights. *The Accountant's House* throws light on the spirit of the Chinese people: their manners, their hospitality, their hardships, and their fortitude. *Research in Jiangsu Province* is a poem in which Seth's background in Economics directly contributes to the form. The poem is rendered statistically, in ironic contrast to the life it depicts, and takes a dig at the meaningless and inaccurate collection of economic data. The poet feels that he would learn things of far more value by imbibing the spirit of the place and by getting to really know the people who are now merely furnishers of economic data for his doctoral research in economics.

There are two love poems—*From a Traveler*, and *A Little Distance*. The former is a highly allusive requiem for love left behind in California, while the latter explores a relationship that by mutual consent has become restricted to platonicity for a while.

All these poems display an undercurrent of serenity that runs deep. There is in them a certain meditative quality that reveals a soul that has found contentment with its life at that point in time. The poet has the leisure to linger at the various gardens, reflect on the culture of the city, enjoy the music of the erhu played by an old stranger.

The 'Neem' section reflecting on Seth's Indian heritage is primarily autobiographical. The poet is on home turf and in *The Comfortable Classes at Work and Play*, he portrays a morning in the life of the Seth family, including the family dog, the flowers in the garden, and even the peacocks in the neighboring house in the portrait:

A squirrel crawls on top of Ganesh,
Oscar turns over on his stomach and rolls about.
Seven satbhai-champas chatter and burble
Below the begonia trellis.
The raat-ki-rani and harsingar
Mingle their scent.
Above, two crows in the eaves upset Diwali
Diyas on the ground, And in the evening a hoopoe pecks at the lawn
While mynahs frolic at the edge of the mango's shade
And parrots flash across the sky [...] (29).

Seth devotes an octet to each member of his family, and in the eight lines, manages to pinpoint each one's *raison d'etre* completely. The poem thus makes very interesting reading as an autobiographical piece.

Homeless voices the uncertainty inherent in moving from one rented house to another. The poem is the fruit of one of Seth's deeper meditations:

A place on the earth untenured,
Soil, grass, brick, air;
To know I will never have to move;
To review the seasons from one lair.
When night comes, to lie down in peace;
To know that I may die as I have slept;
That things will not revert to a stranger's hand;
That those I love may keep what I have kept (34).

Three other poems—*Profiting*, *The They*, and *The Gift*, stand apart as attempts to identify with another's pain or lifestyle. The final poem in this section is from the Babur-Nama: *Memoirs of Babur, First Moghul Emperor of India*, which is a poetical rendition of some of the episodes in the prose autobiography of Babur. The poems in this section, for the most part, betray an uneasy restlessness, prompted by the misery that Seth sees around him.

The poems in 'Live-Oak' have all been written during Seth's stay in California, where, as Seth says, he found out how to have fun. He found friends, love, and laughter; but there was also uncertainty, a feeling of rootless-ness, of not quite belonging, that come with cultural displacement. The poems in this section are thus a mixed lot, and several of them evoke neither sadness nor joy—they are just spaced-out accounts of Seth's days. *Curious Mishaps*, *Waiting*, *And Some Have Madness thrust Upon Them*, *Abalone Soup*—all belong to this category. *And Some Have Madness Thrust Upon Them* reveals the somewhat amusing face of American consumerism, while *Abalone Soup* portrays an aspect of California life in vivid detail. Poems betraying the loneliness in Seth's soul on account of living in a foreign land are *Coast Starlight*, *Love and Work*, and *Ceasing Upon the Midnight*.

Coast Starlight concludes with the haunting cadence of these lines: "O travelers, may starlight see you home/O travelers, may you not sleep alone" (46). *Love and Work* is written in a similar vein, reflecting the ennui that comes through living a life devoid of any meaning due to the lack of the stabilizing anchor that love and friendship provide. The poem ends on a note of uncharacteristic pessimism:

[...] There is so much to do
There isn't any time for feeling blue
There isn't any time for feeling sad.
Things could be worse. Right now they're only bad (62).

Ceasing Upon the Midnight has an obvious parallel in Keats' *Ode to A Nightingale*. Seth is in the same suicidal mood, but throughout the poem there is the tacit understanding that the poet is far too sane to actually do such a thing. He just toys with the idea for a while, decides that his room, with its phone-rings, fridge noises, and other ticks and hums, would "make an unpacific tomb" (63). So he goes outdoors to "cease upon the midnight" (63), playfully cherishing his glum mood:

[...] Ah, tonight,
How rich it seems to be
Alive unhappily [...] (63).

The poem is an exercise in a searching for an identity that transcends geographical barriers. In apt simile, Seth compares his life to an aimless meandering:

[...] Down a dead river on a plain,
Null, unhorizoned, whose terrain,
Devoid of entity, leads to no open sea [...] (65).

As in the Keatsian original, Seth too has been drinking and reminiscing on what seems to him a futile existence. However, he soon finds his funny bone again, and as a grey owl hoots in the night, "He imitates the cries/Chants shreds, invents replies" (65). A drinking bout in the open air, reading poetry, soon clears his head and the inanity of his grief comes home to him. He concludes:

[...] The alcohol, his molecules,
The clean and intimate air, the rules
Of meter, shield him from
Himself. To cease upon
The midnight under the live-oak
Seems too derisory a joke.

The bottle lies on the ground.
He sleeps. His sleep is sound (65).

By having written this poem in the third person, Seth cleverly saves it from becoming solipsistic. In an indirect, inoffensive manner, personal issues are discreetly dealt with and laid to rest.

There is only one pure Nature piece in this section—*Between Storms*, which is an artistic portrayal of storm season in California.

All the other poems in this section are love poems: *From California*, *Spring of Content*, *Moonlight*, *Unclaimed*. *From California* is a coming-to-terms with love that has passed, and the poem highlights Seth's keen sensitivity. *Spring of Content* basks in the sunshine of love shared and the happiness it bestows, reflected in the keen eye for Nature. *Moonlight* is an exquisite poem mourning the loss of love, and accentuating the fact that even time, the great healer, can never fully assuage the pain in the poet's heart. Seth says, "The moon tonight/

Sears with a fire new time and loves won't douse" (56). *Unclaimed* delves into the realm of loveless lovemaking, where no hopes and expectations are shared, and correspondingly, no pain is shared as well.

These are the poems in *The Humble Administrator's Garden*. China provides the predominant influence (hence the title), followed by California, and then India. The poems in the section inspired by China (Wu-tong) reveal Seth to be at the zenith of his peace. California arouses too much restlessness in him with its alienness and reminds him of lost love; India, with all it poverty and misery, weighs heavy on his sensitive soul. It is only in China that Seth is too moved by the stillness, the absolute quietude of nature, to be perturbed by more worldly concerns.

III. ALL YOU WHO SLEEP TONIGHT

There are clear thematic demarcations in this book as well. This volume comes on the heels of Seth's verse-novel, *The Golden Gate*. In *All You Who Sleep Tonight* Seth once again displays his remarkable facility for putting the exact felt emotion into words. X.J. Kennedy writes about this book, "Clear as a glacial pool, often as deep, Vikram Seth's new poems shine with unfashionable virtues. Set gives joy by writing brilliantly well, unafraid to feel and to start us feeling."[10] These words epitomize all thc salient features of this collection. These poems are also the most representative of Seth's oeuvre because all of his characteristic themes—memory, detachment, exile—and styles, from translations to epigrams, are present here.

Romantic Residues consists of poems that are exactly what the title suggests: love lost, remembered, pondered on, dissected and analyzed, and finally laid to rest. There is a tender reaching out to touch the fabric of lost love. *Round and Round*, *Protocols*, *Across*, *Mistaken*, *The Room and the Street*, *Walk*—all dwell on the theme of altercations, of boundaries crossed, of mutual pain and of shared memories. When Seth writes about love lost it is almost when he has distanced himself enough to dissociate himself from love's hurt and pain, only feeling a remaining human sympathy. Thus he says in Across:

Across these miles I wish you well.
May nothing haunt your heart but sleep.
May you not sense what I don't tell.
May you not dream, or doubt, or weep.
May what my pen this peaceless day
Writes on this page not reach your view
Till its deferred print lets you say
It speaks to someone else than you.[11]

Mistaken is another poem that analyses estrangement. *The Room and the Street* talks about the brashness involved in consciously ending a relationship that has turned sour, and *Walk* speaks of shared memories of things which have ceased to exist in the present context of time. *A Style of Loving* is a take-off on the John-Janet relationship in *The Golden Gate*. The sentiment expressed is that it is better not to love, rather than to love and lose. Love, with all its complications, is not for the fainthearted, and though Seth does not shrink from the commitment that love demands, he is at the phase in his life where friendship has more to offer than passion. He asks:

[...] Were we to become lovers
Where would our best friends be?
You do not wish, nor I
To risk again
This savored light for noon's
High joy or pain (15).

Friendship thus seems a safer, if less rewarding proposition.

Sit is a poem that takes a sardonic look at the frenzied, yet aimless pace of modern life. In the feverish preoccupation with the good life, luxuries, money, the years of one's life are squandered away irrevocably. It is only an old timer, who, having seen the world and the way it works, and who is now out of the rat race, can say to the less enlightened:

[...] The world is too opaque, distressing, and profound.
This twenty-minutes' rendezvous will make my day.

> To sit here in the sun, with grackles all around, Staring with beady eyes, and you two feet away (19).

The emphasis is on human bonding, which has become a casualty to a fast-paced life.

Reading all these poems is a valuable lesson in experiencing the many undertones that love can assume; an emotion that is so oft wielded with gusto in the face of parents and the rest of the world, but seldom comprehended by youngsters. Naturally, Seth does not seek to provide tutorials on how one should love —yet, he does so inadvertently, through his love poetry. Love is the stronghold of his existence, so he can never be flippant about it, and this is what comes through in these poems.

In Other Voices acknowledges three specific influences—*Ghalib: Life and Letters* (Ralph Russel and Kurshid Islam), Harvard University Press; *Commandant of Auschwitz* (Rudolf Hoess), Weidenfeld; *Hiroshima Diary* (Michikito Hachiya), University of North Carolina Press. There is something to be said for Seth's clairsentience. In these poems he gets under the skin of other people at several moments in the making of history and tries to fathom what it must have been like to witness the horrors of Auschwitz or to live through the bombing of Hiroshima, among others.

To Wei Ba, Who has lived Away from the Court is a translation from the Chinese of Du Fu; the account is poignant due to the ephemeral nature of the meeting between two friends. *Lithuania: Questions and Answers*, *Work and Freedom*, and *A Doctor's Journal Entry for August 6, 1945* form a trilogy recounting war horrors as seen through the eyes of those who have witnessed them firsthand. *Lithuania: Questions and Answers* underlines the barbarity of war, specially the plight of women; *Work and Freedom* recounts life at one of the most infamous concentration camps—Auschwitz; *A Doctor's* [...] relives the bombing of Hiroshima. In this poem, the use of the journal form as a reporting device is ingenious because it dispenses with the necessity of using rhyme, and the clipped, colloquial style is in keeping with the somber theme.

Ghalib, Two Years after the Mutiny goes back to colonial times and the plight of the Urdu poet Mirza Ghalib, after the mutiny of 1857.

Soon voices the thoughts of a person who is critically ill with a terminal disease, and who knows that death is but a breath away. The poem expresses the universal human sentiment to hold on to life:

[...] Stand by my steel ward bed
And hold me where I lie,
Love me when I am dead
And do not let me die (35).

The poems in *In Other Places* describe Nature as observed by Seth in different geographical locations spread throughout the world. *Hill Dawn* opens to a clear, fresh, pre-dawn hour in the mountains of Garhwal. *Suzhou Park* is a good example of Seth's style, which is so graphic that every little detail is captured, the emphasis falling on visual perception:

Magnolia trees float out their flowers,
Vast, soft, upon a rubbish heap.
The grandfather sits still for hours;
His lap-held grandson is asleep.
Above him plane trees fan the sky.
Nearby, a man in muted dance
Does tai-qi-quan. A butterfly
Flies whitely past his easy trance.
A magpie flaps back to its pine.
A sparrow dust-rolls, fluffs, and cheeps.
The humans rest in a design:
One writes, one thinks, one moves, one sleeps,
The leaves trace out the stenciled stone,
And each is in his dream alone (40).

Night in Jiangning, a poem of only eight limes, invokes a contentment, a willingness to accept life, that lesser poets cannot achieve even in twenty. *Lion Grove, Suzhou* reveals the way in which Seth voices oft-felt but seldom expressed emotions. *Tourists* is a passing observation on the way the world changes. *Qingdago: December* is suffused with the calm that

Mother Nature evokes in Seth, lifting him into a saner, quieter world. *On the Fiftieth Anniversary of the Golden Gate Bridge* recounts the various setbacks after which San Francisco's great landmark finally bridged the gap between Marin and San Francisco and highlights the significance that the bridge has achieved over the years, both as a symbol of man taming the forces of Nature, as well as a place for humans to find whatever it is they are searching for. *The Scent of Sage and Bay*, the final poem in this section, is set in California and is a pure Nature piece.

The eponymously titled *Quatrains* consists of poems that are brilliant little gems, crystallizing Seth's wit, humor, eye for picturesque detail, and his emotions—love, pain, and an impalpable reaching out to grasp something he is not sure is even there. Some of the quatrains analyze the complexity of life, ending in a sudden epiphany:

PENDULUM

The nervous mother shouting ceaselessly
At her roped children swinging from the tree
Remembers with a start she once was young
And terrified her mother as she swung (57).

Some quatrains are just brilliantly comic:

MALEFIC THINGS

Imagining the flower-pot attacked it,
The kitten flung the violets near and far.
And yet, who knows? This morning as I backed it,
My car was set upon by a parked car. (58)

Meditations of the Heart contains poems that are deeply reflective, although one or two are just descriptions of some of Vikram's day-to-day life. *The Stray Cat*, *The Wind* are such. *Poet* and *Adagio* stand alone. *Poet* describes the imprisonment of Irina Ratushinkaya. *Adagio* is a tribute to the musical genius of Mozart. *Mist* is a reassessing of human expectations and motives. *How Rarely these Few Years* begins on a subjective note but goes on to express a universal human fear:

How rarely these few years, as work keeps us aloof,
Or fares, or one thing or another,
Have we had days to spend under our parents' roof:
Myself, my sister, and my brother.

All five of us will die; to reckon from the past
This flesh and blood is unforgiving.
What's hard is that just one of us will be the last
To bear it all and go on living (70).

Things dissects the idiosyncratic nature of the world and the way in which it works. *Voices* looks at the rat race that life has become. *Heart* looks for meaning in the everyday working of the human body. The closing poem in this section, *All You Who Sleep Tonight*, is an exquisite pearl. It is addressed to travellers all over the world and goes thus:

All you who sleep tonight
Far from the ones you love,
No hand to left or right,
And emptiness above—

Know that you aren't alone
The whole world shares your tears,
Some for two nights or one,
And some for all their years (76).

Apart from the connotation of expatriation, the salient feature of the poem is that in it life is reproduced in the simplest of words but rendered with a poignancy that brings a tear to the eye and a catch to the throat.

As regards Seth's poetic technique it can be said that his insistence on the directness of utterance and his harnessing of razor-sharp images as a means to achieve cohesion and coherence makes his style uniquely sensitive. Also, the variety in his verse characterizes his exploration of suitable verse forms for his experiences, and reveals his ability to handle adroitly different kinds of verse.

Seth is in kinship with the neo-modernists in so far as his concerns and preoccupations range from introspection and self-analysis, to recollected personal emotion, from expressions of involvement in the social milieu, to those of extreme isolationist attitudes and a wrestling with one's own inner self to come to terms with it. As a modern poet, Seth has no use for the poetic inversions of Toru Dutt or the saccharine sweetness of Sarojini Naidu's poetry. To him, the poem itself is a mode for experiencing language. In all the above respects Seth is modern. Yet, he upholds tradition and acknowledges his literary influences with a candidness that is disarming, considering the paranoia other writers exhibit when asked about their influences. Devesh Patel states that "Seth is an anachronism in a poetic arena known for its strangely in-bred and solipsistic characteristics."[12] He is more interested in the world outside than on the intricacies of his own sensibility. Also, his poetry rhymes and uses older forms, demonstrating an impressive reading and poetic vocabulary. Secondly, there is no confessional neurosis in his poetry. The most noteworthy thing is that Seth's poetry resembles some of the best productions of the English tradition technically, and augments them with the varied experiences of Seth's self-styled exile.[13]

Seth's treatment of Nature in his poetry merits special analysis. In his Nature portrayal, Seth is in affinity with the Romantics. Like Wordsworth, Keats, and Tennyson, he writes with his eye steadily fixed upon his object. His emotional response to Nature is quiet and balanced. The stillness of a pond, the turning of a leaf, the ripples made by the wind on the surface of water; he stands, unobtrusive, content to paint in words what his eye sees. His Nature poetry in not a backdrop for human pageants: man and Nature exist as separate entities, and if Nature does play a part, it is that of still and silent spectator. Further, the delight that Seth experiences in Nature is not "that simple, spontaneous, unreflecting pleasure which all unsophisticated beings feel in free open-air life."[14] His enjoyment of Nature is intellectual and systematic. He has to know the name of every tree that he describes, every flower that catches his eye, and every fish that swims past him. This kind of sensuous apprehension of Nature, that has no need of "any interest unborrowed from the eye,"[15] envisages a love for Nature sans any mystical or spiritual connotations. In this respect, Seth is most near to

Keats. To Keats, a flower is a flower; it does not speak to him of eternity or arouse mystical wonder in him, as it would have with Wordsworth or Tennyson. He is content to merely enjoy it in its sensuous beauty. It is likewise with Seth. For the most part, no disturbing sentiments affect his moments with Nature.

A thematic study of Seth's poetry seems to postulate that love posited in friendship is the more durable substratum of human life, as compared to the "high joy or pain" that true love brings. This sentiment is more deeply explored in *The Golden Gate*, first in the John—Janet relationship and later in the Phil-Liz one, and later in *A Suitable Boy*, in Lata's choice of a husband. But it would be presumptuous to believe that Seth truly feels this. He merely toys with the idea for a while, when love has brought him too much pain, but ultimately realizes that love cannot be reduced to a matter of convenience or a comfortable adjustment between two people. This conclusion is borne out by Seth's poems themselves, for in them, there is no mistaking the way Seth yearns for love lost, the unbridled delight with which he cherishes love found—this is not the "savoured light" that is temporarily easy on the eye but truly "noon's high joy or pain" that lights up his life.

These three volumes of poetry reveal Seth, the man, in a way that his novels do not, despite the fact that they are far lengthier. This is because Seth's poetry is the poetry of personal association and is therefore of an individual rather than of a general character. In contrast, his novels have very little of him. In his poetry, Seth deals with personal issues like cultural displacement, love, loss, pain, and other emotions so that they no longer trouble him, as he later writes his novels.

A few poems in these collections are banal, in particular the translations, although the reader can, of course, force himself to appreciate the sentiment behind them: that of bringing to the reader who is unfamiliar with these languages something of the beauty which would be inaccessible otherwise, but such poems are few and far between. One only wishes that Seth had used a more ruthless pair of editorial scissors, a shortcoming that mars these collections to a certain extent, despite all their merits. In the final analysis however, these collections are praiseworthy, not only because they reveal Seth's ability to handle different kinds of verse but also because these poems are embodiments of the oft sidelined fact that the primary aim in doing creative work of any kind, (in Seth's case writing poetry) is for one's own pleasure. These poems were written primarily for that very old fashioned reason: the sheer joy of writing. Some of these poems fulfil the need for catharsis, some take a sardonic (though urbane) look at the drama of human life; but for the most part they are heartfelt and spontaneous outbreaks into a language of delight. This natural pleasure filters through to the poems themselves. This fact, coupled with the unmistakable emotion in these poems, gives a pleasure that will make the reader return to them again and again.

Notes

1. Interview by Katherine Knorr, "Vikram Seth Plays to his Truest Judges," *International Herald Tribune* Online Edition, Apr 4, 1999.
2. "Introduction," *The Poems* 1981-1994, Penguin Books India, 1995, xiv.
3. Cynthia Haven, "Poetic Licence," *Stanford Magazine* (May/June 1999).
4. *Ibid.*
5. Knorr, *ibid.*
6. C. Paul Verghese, *Essays on Indian Writing in English*, N.V. Publications, Delhi, 1975, 47.
7. Introduction to *Mappings*,Viking Penguin India, 1994, x.
8. Ruth Morse, *Rooted Cosmopolite: Vikram Seth And 'The Scars of Middlemarch.'* Fitzwilliam College, Cambridge. URL:www.perso.worldonline.fr/ebc/s.html.
9. Donald Davie, review of The Humble Administrator's Garden, Front Flap, Penguin India, 1994.
10. X.J. Kennedy, Book Review at amazon.com.
11. *All You Who Sleep Tonight*, Penguin Books India, 1990, 16
12. Devesh Patel, "Poetry of an Exile," *Contemporary Poetry Review*. URL:www.webdelsol.com/CPR/Patel/Vikram.htm
13. *Ibid.*
14. William H. Hudson, *An Introduction to the Study of Literature*, George Harrap and Co. Great Britain, 1910, 321
15. *Ibid.*

3

The Ambition for an Elaborate Expression: *The Golden Gate*

The Golden Gate occupies the watershed position in Vikram Seth's life. The inspiration for the novel was Pushkin's *Eugene Onegin*.[1] After reading *Onegin*, Seth realized that he had found a medium for the story he had been wanting to tell about California. In reading *Onegin*, three things came together: the idea of the novel, the actual structure and the classical structure of the stanzas, and the idea of writing about California and life in California, because Seth was studying there at the time. The basic theme of the novel was provided by a lunch meeting with a friend, a Japanese-American woman. Their discussion of their then rather unsuccessful love lives became the opening scene of *The Golden Gate*.

This "whole passé extravaganza,"[2] as Seth mocks, was met with scepticism by publishers, editors, and friends alike. In an authorial intrusion in the novel, Seth describes the reaction of a publisher:

> [...] "Dear fellow,
> What's your next work?" "A Novel [...]" "Great!
> We hope that you, dear Mr. Seth—"
> "[...] In verse," I added. He turned yellow.
> "How marvellously quaint," he said,
> And subsequently cut me dead [...] (100).

But Seth's tour-de-force is far from being a misguided attempt at professional hara-kiri. The strength of the book lies in the fact that the issues it treats of are those that will not pass away with time; the book will continue to speak to each successive generation.

The theme of the novel is one of the classic materials of all comedy—man's search for love—and the various mishaps that befall him in the course of that search, although the rest of the novel leads less to the traditional comic ending (nuptials all around), than to surprising sadness. The novel begins from this relatively simple inception and steadily enlarges in scope as it becomes a bittersweet love story, a wickedly funny novel of manners, and an unsentimental meditation on morality and the nuclear abyss.

John Brown, the hero, is a Silicon Valley computer professional who's highly successful career stands in abysmal contrast to his personal life, which leaves much to be desired. When he gets hit hard by a frisbee while taking a walk, he thinks:

> [...] If I died, who'd be sad?
> Who'd weep? Who would be glad?
> Would anybody? (3).

This dismal rumination is not in the nature of paranoid self-pity; it is a cold-blooded evaluation of the state of affairs in John's world. John is an emotional non-entity. Nobody needs him beyond his work, and this irks him no end. Beneath all his frivolent capers and his outward aggressiveness, he has the basic human need to be loved by somebody. He uncomfortably senses that he exists in a vacuum, while around him life is passing him by. He knows that he is "a linkless node, no spouse or sibling/No children [...]" (6). Nothing offers solace anymore—not books, or music, nor any of the things he enjoyed doing earlier. His only female friend is Janet Hayakawa, erstwhile lover, now, through mutual agreement (prompted by a neurotic compulsion to avoid a permanent relationship), the two share a friendship that is shielded "from all passion" (8).

When the two meet for lunch, John pours out his woes to her. Janet astutely diagnoses that the remedy to John's problems is to be in a stable relationship. Her proposal that John advertise for a potential life-mate is met with horror by John, who declares that he will not demean himself in this manner. However, Janet takes matters into her own hands by advertising for John. Out of the deluge of letters that arrive, John selects three, but nothing comes of them. More letters arrive later and out of these John selects one he likes—that of Elizabeth Dorati. The two meet, hit it off instantly, and fall in love.

The story now shifts to focus on Phil Weiss, a college friend of John and fellow computer professional. Phil has given up a promising career in nuclear science to become an environmentalist. He has a son, Paul, whom he is raising all alone, because he has become estranged from his wife, Claire. Phil runs into John and Liz at a music concert, in which Liz's sister, Sue, is performing. Having renewed their acquaintance, Phil gets invited to John and Liz's house-warming party, where he meets Ed, Liz's brother. The two indulge in a homosexual relationship, but as Ed feels guilty about homosexuality on ethical grounds, their liaison is plagued by uncertainty and denial.

In the meantime, things are not going so well for John and Liz either. Charlemagne, Liz's cat, detests John with a vengeance, and makes his life miserable in all the ways cats can. But Liz is not ready to part with him, even for John's sake. She has also learned of the affair between her brother and Phil and has accepted it, but this becomes a major bone-of-contention with John, who is disgusted and censorious and breaks off all contact with Phil. The situation becomes explosive when the two are holidaying at Liz's parents' place. John proposes to Liz, but contrary to his expectations, she does not immediately accept. John is surprised and a little hurt, but decides to give Liz more time. However, when he sees a letter from Phil in Liz's hand, he rashly concludes that she is cheating on him and ends their affair. Phil and Liz now get married, not because they are in love but because they have both realized that companionship is a more solid foundation for marriage than passion.

Meanwhile, John, alone again, rediscovers his friendship with Janet, and reawakens to the love he had always felt for her. But as fate would have it, just when they are on the verge of committing to each other, Janet dies in an accident, and John is left heartbroken and bereft. The story closes with Janet's words ringing in John's ears:

> [...] I'm with you John. You're not alone.
> Trust me my friend; there is the phone.
> It isn't me you are obeying.
> Pay what are your own hearts arrears.
> Now clear your throat; and dry these tears (307).

There is thus the tacit understanding that John will pick up the pieces of his life and will renew human contact by breaking down his wall of isolation, thereby returning to sanity and normalcy.

The basic theme is thus that of isolation and estrangement. Exploring the alienation in modern American society, Trilling says, "[...] the individual is not only isolated from society, he is isolated from everyone he knows, even his own love partner."[3] Seth unflinchingly presents this malady afflicting modern society: the morbid preoccupation with one's own affairs to the exclusion of everything and everyone else, the selfishness inherent in the non-sharing of thoughts, time, and needs, the stubborn rejection of human bonding: in essence, the problem confronting modern urban society is that in it all the things that constitute the very structure of society have been torn down.

John best exemplifies this dilemma of modern man. He has all he could want in terms of material acquisitions, is handsome, smart, well mannered, well read—in essence, the perfect companion, and yet he is lost and lonely. Seth presents the pathology behind this: in his carefree youth, John has not given love the attention it deserves, preferring the freedom that bachelorhood connotes to most men to the shackles of matrimony. Not only John but most American men and women are equally unwilling to sacrifice what they perceive as their freedom, by committing to a permanent relationship.

John and Janet break off their liaison as soon as it shows signs of developing into something serious. Claire abandons Phil without a second thought under the feeble pretext of his dominating nature. This fanatic obsession for keeping the heart aloof from the rest of the body lies at the root of the problem. In psychological terms this is known as 'relationship anxiety'—the refusal to grow into a mature relationship. Almost every major character in the novel suffers from this anxiety and John most of all. Although both John and Janet are making earnest attempts to get over this anxiety in the course of the novel, when Janet dies it is suddenly too late for them. Phil and Liz are the only ones who do not suffer from it and appropriately, they are the ones rewarded with secure, happy lives. Apart from Phil and Liz, the other characters somehow fail to realize that the security provided by a permanent relationship cannot be replaced by an outwardly successful life, and that pets can never fully substitute the warmth of human bonding. Ed's anxiety is of a different kind; he wants the heart without the body to keep his soul guiltless, but does not want to face the fact that this is not what he really wants.

However, all the characters, deep down beneath their facades of self-sufficiency and modernity, crave the basic human desire to be loved. Thus, every major character in the novel is involved in a private odyssey, the quest for that special, earth-shattering love. John has had many flings in his day, but what he really wants is to settle down with somebody he truly loves. He finds that feeling temporarily with Liz and is very content in the interim, until Charlemagne drives them apart. Janet too is holding out for the perfect man, and although she finds that perfection in John, she dies too early for anything to come of it. The quests of Phil and Liz are more complex: each of them has tried romantic love, and both have found it lacking. They would rather settle for companionship, based on shared interests and goals. This quest for love and permanence motivates the actions of the characters.

Another theme in the novel is that of nuclear warfare. Seth expatiates upon the theme unhurriedly, using narration, description, dialogue, sermon, demonstrations, peace marches, even diatribe, to get the point across. Nuclear insanity is a very contemporary theme and it is very significant in this novel because both the theme and the novel are so quintessentially American. America is one of the few countries where people are aware enough to protest the acquisition of nuclear weapons. In the novel, Phil gives up a promising career at Lungless Labs (a place where nuclear bombs are made), to heed his inner voice, which tells him that what he is doing is ethically wrong. Liz participates in the demonstration against the wishes of John, speaking eloquently against the arms race. Father O'Hare sermonizes, proving irrefutably that a nuclear war can only end in total omnicide, and therefore nuclear weapons must never be used. Through all these voices, Seth has devoted considerable time and space to address this issue, brilliantly portraying both sides of the problem in the argument between John and Phil. Seth's view point is unequivocal—he says in the novel, "Nice folks don't use nukes"(152), driving home the fact that such an event spells doom not only for man alone but also for all of Nature's dumb creations, who will unwittingly share man's fate.

Another dominant theme in the novel is that of homosexuality, which makes the novel particularly true to the American way of life. Homosexuality is by no means an American invention but due to its prevalence in American society it has acquired almost a cult status there. Townsend discusses the prevalence of this way of life in America.[4] But *The Golden Gate* is not an attempt to glorify homosexuality. It is true that it is Phil, a homosexual, who is rewarded with a rich family life at the end of the novel, while John has nothing left but memories, but Seth espouses the superiority of personal judgement over any opinions held by convention: "You have a mind too, Ed. Why don't you/Go by what your heart says is right?" (189). It is a credit to Seth's art that neither does the novel glorify homosexuality, nor does it degenerate into a vicious diatribe against it.

The role of American women in modern American society is also important thematically. American women have always shown great enterprise and skill in surviving in the male dominated world; they have been pioneers in every field. It is this independent woman that Seth portrays in the novel. Liz is the epitome of the successful career woman, storming the hitherto Ivy-League bastions of the law firm she works for. And she is not just a dull lawyer—she enjoys music, has a pet cat, and can even deliver an extempore quote-worthy speech about saving the planet from nuclear madmen. Janet represents the artistic side of the American woman—she is drummer and sculptor rolled into one, and has enough confidence in her artistic ability to pursue her career wholeheartedly, even though success has eluded her till now. Through the women characters in the novel, Seth goes deep into the mind of the American woman to discover her personality. Janet and Liz, both have pet cats. Without making an overt statement, Seth indicates that this penchant single American woman have to keep pets is born out of the malaise that afflicts urban America—the alienation from human bonding. Women try to counter their loneliness to some extent by lavishing affection on pets. The American woman also craves the financial security that marriage brings: the deluge of letters that arrive in response to John's advertisement is proof enough. The old values are represented by Liz's mother—but such women are few and far between. The average American woman is a victim of the extreme modernisation of life, and consequently, she is selfish, à la Claire, who leaves Phil for another man without a backward glance, in spite of having a son she is leaving behind. Liz is involved with her career to the extent that love has had no place in her life, despite repeated pleadings from her mother who would like to see her settled down. After the initial flush of love has died down, one finds John complaining that now they (he and Liz) do only those things that Liz wants to do and not the ones that he (John) does.

A natural corollary to the disintegrated persona of the American woman is a dysfunctional family life. As the traditional home maker, it is the woman who keeps the family together, even in today's overlapping and confused roles. But the average American woman is too emancipated to be tied down by any rules, and if her quest for freedom and self satisfaction entails leaving in her wake a trail of broken marriages, broken homes, maladjusted children, then it is a small price to pay. It is through Phil's son Paul that Seth expresses how hard children get hit by estrangement between their parents:

"[...] No Paul, she's gone away." "Forever?"
"I just can't tell you, son, but never
Think you're alone. You've got me." "When
Will you leave me?" Phil, shocked, stares [...] (62).

Being separated from a parent is thus not a bad dream but a fact of life that Paul is just learning to accept.

The family system providing no support, it is natural for people to turn to other social groups, and this is where friendship assumes centre stage. Due to minimal parent-child interaction (a by-product of busy lives), children fulfil their need for affection by bonding with their peers, with whom they spend long hours, at school and at play. The added advantage is that friends are by and large uncensorious, unlike parents. Gradually, friends replace the warmth lacking in familial ties. This type of relationship is beautifully portrayed in *The Golden Gate*. John is lonely, but it is not his mother (who is dead) or his father (who lives half a continent away) that look out for him but his friend Janet. Matt and Joan Lamont name Phil, who is their friend, as their son's guardian in the event of their deaths. John and Phil are bosom buddies until conflicting interests drive them apart. The novel ends on a note emphasizing the importance of friendship: Liz and Phil extend their hands in friendship to John, and John, bereft and lonely, hears Janet's voice in his head, exhorting him to renew the ties of friendship.

Another theme is that of morality. Seth does not subscribe to the concept of conventional Indian morality. As an artist, he recognizes the complexities of human nature, unpalatable though they may be. The moral code presented in the novel is the moral code that America lives by: casual sex is a way of life, as are homosexual relationships, pick-up bars and so on. Social morality, or what one owes to the world at large, has been brought to the forefront by the episode of the peaceful demonstration against Lungless Labs. Seth unambiguously says that one must look beyond one's personal world to do what one can for society as a whole, emphatically stating, "I am my brother's keeper" (152).

These are the various themes that the novel encompasses, and they make the novel so much more than a portrayal of contemporary California life. The theme is the outcome of a deep choice. Seth sees the world around him and it pains him. He sees the mindless striving after materialistic goals, the insatiable greed for everything the world has to offer, the ungoverned lust that is more animal-like than human, the self-centredness, the estrangements from loved ones. But he does not believe in spouting venom against what he perceives as essentially human frailties. He is more compassionate than censorious, more understanding than outraged. In a quiet manner, he strips the glamour from American yuppiedom: there is more to this life than sunshine and California wine—there is loneliness so intense that people build walls around themselves to convince themselves that they are islands, there is self doubt, unrelenting professional pressure, no set of values to live by, confused moral codes, and an ever increasing alienation from the human touch. Seth compels his characters to search for meaning in their lives, and to assume responsibility for their actions instead of blaming the world at large for every thing that goes awry. The novel thus traces the trials and tribulations of John and his circle of friends as they come to terms with their loneliness and several aberrations.

As regards the form, it seems to be the outcome of a judicious choice. As a novel of plot and/or character, *The Golden Gate* is very thin indeed, in essence being little more than a succession of musical beds. To have attempted to render this tale in prose would have produced nothing more then a soap-operatic effect that would hardly have been worthwhile. But the medium Seth has chosen, sequential sonnets, by its very nature calls for a certain dignity of approach as well as it demands from Seth an economy of delineation that ruthlessly leaves out the redundant, allows for a witty couplet at the end of each sonnet to break the monotony, and most importantly, calls attention away from the plot towards the form. Hollinghurst says, "It is truly hard to imagine a better vehicle for social verse narrative, which aims to be both reflective and lightly comic."[5] However, the form is not in the nature of a deliberate volte-face from tradition. The choice is a natural one, considering the fascination that poetry exerts over Seth. Being a poet himself, it was natural for him to turn to a poet for inspiration. The pioneer of the novel in verse was Byron, whose *Don Juan*[6] is a picaresque novel in verse. Pushkin acknowledges Byron as the model for his Eugene Onegin, and likewise, Seth acknowledges Pushkin, in a tribute incorporated into *The Golden Gate*: "Eugene Onegin—like champagne/Its effervescence stirs my brain" (102).

Byron's *Don Juan* is a satire on contemporary European life and civilization. Following Byron, Pushkin created in his novel a realistic portrayal of contemporary Russia. Following their lead, Seth chose to write, both satirically and realistically, a novel about contemporary California. In preparation for writing the novel, Seth read two translations of Pushkin's Onegin, attending especially to the Charles Johnston version, in which the translator followed the Pushkin stanza throughout and approximated to Pushkin's inventiveness in rhyme and rhythm. Pushkin's story was this: young Tatyana loves Eugene Onegin, a Russian noble, and writes him a declaration of her love, but he rejects her. Time passes and several years later Eugene realizes that he loves Tatyana—but by then she is married, in respect and friendship, to someone else, and to whom she intends to remain faithful, even though she admits that she still loves Eugene. The parallels in *The Golden Gate* run as follows: Eugene is reincarnated as John. Among the women, both Liz and Janet correspond to Tatyana in different aspects. Janet has Tatyana's unrequited love and she writes Tatyana's letter, while Liz echoes Tatyana's practical side. The novel follows the structure of *Onegin* throughout. As Pushkin introduced himself into his fictional work as a friend of Onegin, so Seth makes a brief appearance as the anagrammatic Kim Travesh. This is Seth's sole appearance, also like Pushkin.

Seth also imitates Pushkin's presence as a narrator, and like him, tells the reader about the strains of creation in delightful authorial intrusions. The contrast that one finds between the simple country world of Tatyana and that of St. Petersburg and Moscow is paralleled by the portrayal of the vine-growing, simple Dorati family placed in direct opposition to American yuppiedom as represented by John.

The choice of metre that Seth makes is an interesting one, for he says in the novel that the tetrameter, the "once-noble meter," "capers before the proud pentameter, tyrant of English" (3). However, though the pentameter is no doubt stately and grand, the tetrameter has a lilting cadence (as evinced in both Byron and Pushkin) that must have appealed to Seth's musical ear. Pushkin's original consists of about four hundred sonnet-like stanzas written in iambic tetrameter, the rhyming pattern being abab; cdcd; efef; gg. The octave and sestet are usually well defined, although Pushkin leaps across to the next sonnet occasionally to complete a sentence or a thought. But both the tetrameter and the rhyming pattern are followed meticulously throughout. However, the strict defining feature of the Onegin stanzas is the distribution of masculine and feminine rhymes, the pattern running as follows: FMFM; FFMM; FMMFMM. As a result, the lines have a special lilt and sway to them, even in the translated English version. Seth's sonnets retain the octave-sestet division, and due to the conversational tone, appear to be prose sentences, but the use of more feminine rhymes enables the lines to flow into each other seamlessly. The caesura is marked by an elliptical phrase, or a change in the thought.

Seth gets so used to writing in this form that even the acknowledgement, the dedication, and the table of contents have been versified. The opening line is arresting for its humorous dig at the lengthy epic style of yore, which Seth knows the average modern reader is not likely to read. He says: "To make a start more swift than weighty,/Hail Muse! [...]" (1), and plunges into the heart of the tale, making the reader frown, laugh, and cry in a cyclic manifestation of the drama that constitutes the average human life.

Seth is conscious throughout of his "wrinkled muse," "the dusty bread molds of Onegin."(101) This self consciousness is portrayed in the reviewers' attack upon Janet. Fitted into context, the lines would read somewhat like this:

> [...] Miss Hayakawa [Mr. Seth], it appears,
> Lacks serious sculptural [literary] intention.
> Where has she [he] been these thirty years?
> Are Moore's [Rushdie's] and Calder's [Naipaul's] use of medium
> Unknown to her [him]? The languid tedium
> Of lines too fluid to show pains
> Reflect this artist's dated chains:
> Derivative, diluted passion,
> A facile versatility [...] (10).

This is Seth's self-mockery: obsolete form, derivative medium—but Seth is also confident enough to realize the strengths he is aiming for:

> [...] A classic leanness that at length
> Will be applauded for its strength [...]
>
> Such startling sureness and maturity
> And sense of form in one so young [...] (295).

There is undeniably something of all three ('classic leanness,' 'maturity,' and 'sense of form') in Seth's novel, and although it lacks that indefinable spark that makes a classic a 'classic,' the fact that it invites comparison with Pushkin is in itself a considerable achievement. Kaul says:

> What *The Golden Gate* shows is the fine accomplishment that can result when a budding talent commits itself, with joy and inwardness, not to some passing literary fashion or pseudo-profundity, but to the example of a true classic of modern literature.[7]

Coming back to the form, it is such that it successfully links a formal type of poetry with modern moral and spiritual dilemmas. Seth says:

> I realized that one could write about one's own times with a modern sensibility and yet use these forms which have existed in the language for hundreds of years, full of the

resonance they had and the clarity that they almost forced upon one.[8]

The sonnet form is thus harnessed by Seth in a manner that it oscillates from being merely functional in taking the story forward to being rich in poetic eloquence. In the novel, Seth uses the broader base of fiction to unite the two genres of fiction and poetry. By using the stanzaic form innovatively, he "attempts an imaginative and creative union of the two genres so crudely pulled asunder by earlier and lesser writers."[9] This blending is conscious and careful. Realizing the advantages verse wields over prose, Seth uses it to communicate his experiences effectively. This has the added advantage of enabling Seth to use a medium with which he feels comfortable—poetry. His ability to forge an updated and precise medium is in the nature of a vital artistic evolution, leading to a more heightened expression of experience than prose. To have come to actualize such a form, as in Byron and Pushkin, in a contemporary context speaks of the resourcefulness of Seth as a poet. In addition, Seth's novel is faithful to all the pleasing things in the original: his rhymes stun, expressing within them the entire gamut of human emotions—love, hate, ambition, greed, lust, sympathy, dejection—and the novel grows deeper in meaning with every reading, previously veiled nuances of its technical virtuosity coming to light.

The title Seth has chosen is of special import, because the name The Golden Gate Bridge captures the quintessence of modern California. It stands as a defining feature of America's west coast, just as the Statue of Liberty is the defining feature of the eastern one. In the novel, Seth uses the bridge to indicate the setting of his tale, and the identifying landmark of San Francisco becomes the novel's *raison d'etre* as well, becoming the majestic backdrop of the human drama that unfolds.

However, the bridge is more than just an identifying feature of Seth's tale. In ancient alchemy, the element corresponding to the emotion of love was gold; gold, the metal that stands for all that is pure and worthwhile in human life. The Golden Gate Bridge, with all its connotations of the material of which it is a namesake, is thus the concrete image of human love reaching out and connecting people. The bridge becomes a symbol of love, representative of the soul test of worthiness, which all the characters must traverse before being let into the sanctum sanctorum of the kind of love they have only ever dreamed about, never known. Janet, with her broad human sympathy, has already crossed it, as have Phil and Liz, in their own compassionate way. John learns the lesson last of all, as Janet's voice calls to him from beyond the grave. The bridge is thus an apt symbol of the effort each one must make to reach out and connect with the rest of one's fellow beings. Seth says in the novel:

> [...] In life's brief game to be a winner
> A man must have [...] O yes, above
> All else, of course, someone to love [...] (129).

Love is elusive, because it means different things to different people. For John and Janet, it is all or nothing at all, for Phil and Liz, sadder but wiser, it is a comfortable sharing of trust, mutual respect, loyalty and friendship. For Ed love is an abstraction linking him to God and to his own soul. Seth's basic premise is that love is a vital, life giving force; that it is possible to exist without love but only in an inhuman, vegetable kind of way.

Love in a broader context is evinced by Father O'Hare's crusade against nuclear research, embodying man's concern for his fellowmen and for the environment in which he co-habits with all of creation. Maternal love is exemplified in Mrs. Marie Dorati, and paternal love in Phil. In all these visions of love, Seth's motto rings true: love is the medium by means of which man can redeem his life. He recalls the reader to sanity and old-fashioned values, the cornerstones of which are family and a general human sympathy. The modern day wasteland that is man's legacy may still be reclaimed, if the gentle showers of love and compassion fall upon it. The novel charts the progress of each character from selfishness and rigidity to concern and caring. By the end of the novel, most of them, even Charlemagne the cat, have traversed the Golden Gate Bridge symbolically, and grown.

As regards the tone of the novel, it is light-hearted and parodic. It "creates a complex web of sense and sensibility on various levels that ultimately results in extremely sophisticated parody."[10] Parody is present in the choice and elaboration of form and theme, in style, treatment, and technique. It thus operates at the structural level in the novel. The opening lines of the novel serve to illustrate:

To make a start more swift than weighty,
Hail muse. Dear reader, once upon
A time, say, circa 1980,
There lived a man. His name was John [...] (3).

These lines evoke the traditional epical invocation. "Dear reader" imitates the epistolatory origins of the early eighteenth century novel, and "once upon a time" follows the oral folk cultural traditions. The parody goes on to create inter textuality, not only of cross referential cultural connotations but also subtle inter textuality of literary style and forms.

An analysis of the novel reveals that it is conceived in a spirit of humour coupled with rebellious irony. This is brought about by the selective facts that Seth highlights about the characters. His style of sparse verse serves him well here. The characters are presented only in vignettes and as they push the story forward, Seth adds a touch of sardonic humour by inserting the authorial voice in parenthesis: "Friends claim he's grown aloof and prim./(His boss, though, is well pleased with him)" (4), or "As did Phil too, until his recent/flight from the rich realms of Defence/(With what John holds to be indecent/ Precipitation and bad sense)" (8). This style is ideal, both for the medium, which demands brevity, and for the theme, which demands levity and wit to keep it from sinking into a maudlin formlessness. Seth's wit is razor-sharp, and commendably, it never crosses the boundaries of good taste. The description of the cacophony paraded as music by Janet's rock band "Liquid Sheep," is an apt illustration of Seth's technique:

[...] She is the drummer in a band
Well known and feared throughout the city:
The striking sounds of Liquid Sheep

Rouse distant suburbs from their sleep.
Unlinked, alike to tune or ditty,
Their music is a throttled yelp—
Morse crossed with a pig's squeal for help [...] (9).

The humour is also achieved by the use of anticlimax, anti thesis, and other figures of speech. Sometimes Seth creates humour by emphasizing some small insignificant detail, as for instance:

[...] You need a lover, John, I think.
Someone I'd say, who's fun to be with—
And, of course, vitamin C to eat—
And chooses a richer lens to see with
.. . .
The fervour of her declamation
Induces her to drum a roll
With her chopsticks upon her bowl [...] (15).

The humour in the novel is predominantly of this kind—the humour of situation coupled with the somewhat endearing neuroticism of the characters. The replies that John gets in response to his advertisement, his description of the mess that is his life, Charlemagne's campaign to oust John from his domain and John's mounting helplessness, Ed and his pet iguana, even the description of John and Liz in the first flush of love: all these episodes provide Seth with an opportunity to display his wit, and make the novel irresistibly funny. The paradox is that the story is not light-toned—only its treatment is such. But it is not in Seth's repertoire to churn out page after page of unyielding gravity. Seth's style cannot be detached from his humour. It becomes clear that the froufrou atmosphere that Seth conjures up is an effective medium, especially in a novel in which a severe treatment of the course of events could only have resulted in an unbearably heavy tale. By being comic, Seth alleviates the gloom of the dire sequence of events, simultaneously paving the way for his exposition on nuclear issues and the value of friendship and family.

As regards characterisation in the novel, the characters are not full fledged portraits—they are thumbnail sketches. A minor stroke here, a quick brush there; physical attributes are almost absent. For instance, all the reader knows of John is that he is tall and good looking; Liz has blue eyes and one knows little else. This is a trend which continues in Seth's later work as well, presumably because describing physical attributes seems to Seth to be an unprofitable exercise, concerned as he is with the mental makeup of his characters rather than with the physical. But in this novel, Seth is not too intent on portraying the inner life of his characters either. He just tells the tale, and leaves it to the reader to form conceptions about the characters; the implied reading being that that there is a vital connection between the thought processes of each character and his or her actions. This is the reason that in spite of being mere vignettes, the characters are all well rounded.

The male characters are less flatteringly portrayed than the female ones; they are confused and helpless in the face of their problems, whereas the females are competent, full blooded, and talented, and emotionally and psychologically much stronger and mature. Liz does suffer from an eating disorder and Janet does feel that her life is a mess, yet the female characters emerge as more well rounded personalities, compared to the complex—ridden, egoistical, and guilt ridden behaviour of the males. Even Claire, who does not appear before the reader directly, is given an aura of class and nobility that seems to be beyond the ken of the simple Phil.

Interrelationships among characters are also interestingly portrayed. The gay relationship that Phil and Ed share has a high level of complexity that does not get sorted out with time. On the other hand, the relationship between Phil and Liz has a complex simplicity based on shared goals in life, even though they both are intrinsically very different. John's relationship with Janet exists on several different levels. The two are friends, erstwhile lovers, each other's best critics, and ultimately, they realize that they are soul mates.

Seth's characters are living in a world where sentimentality is taken to be a moronic trait. Yet, John is "tender beneath a carapace" (5), and before he learned to be self-involved, the city of San Francisco had a special place in his heart. Seeking refuge in other activities had worked earlier, but lately nothing can tune out the loneliness that is consuming him. Janet is similarly lonely:

> [...] Jan relishes the warmth and savour
> The deeds of Cuff and Kink confer,
> The love they deign to yield to her [...] (11).

Janet knows that John's vision of life is a lopsided one: he tends not to see things in their perspective and blows them out of all proportion. He is not broadminded enough to tolerate change or difference of opinion. Janet recognizes the predicament they are all in:

> [...] The loneliness within our souls,
> Our febrile clawing for mean goals,
> Our programmed cockfights and rat races,
> Our dreary dignity, false pride,
> And hearts stored in formaldehyde [...] (20).

There is no doubt that John's emotional rigidity is justifiable; it can be traced back to his disturbed childhood and the lack of a mother's stabilizing love. He has learned to be self sufficient, but solitude is the one thing he cannot handle. When he meets Liz, her compassion and warmth melt away all his emotional barriers. Their housewarming is John's most cherished dream come true—it is all he has ever striven for, initially on a subconscious level, and later, as he comes to terms with his loneliness, with conscious acceptance. He is "warmed by the solace of arrival:/A loner who at last has come/In a new house, to a new home" (129). When things turn sour with Liz, John is totally at his wits' end. His world seems to him a large void that nothing can ever fill up again. This is coupled with his sense of outrage, first at the discovery that his best friend is a homosexual, and second that Liz jilts him and chooses Phil: these two events affect him too deeply for him to stay balanced. He cannot quite believe that the two people he loves most should so thoroughly fall short of the expectations he has from them. The lesson Seth expresses is this: the perfect idols our minds build up do not exist, and instead of trying to make others conform to our expectations so that one may find it easier to love them, one ought to make an effort to adjust with other people as proof of one's love. Every relationship has a chance of succeeding if people are willing to make changes in themselves, instead of just opting out of the relationship when things start to get sticky: "While those who wait, as age advances/Aloof for Ms. or Mr. Right/ Weep to themselves in the still night" (21).

In a verse narrative the emphasis usually falls on the sequence of events rather than on character, but Seth makes his characters lifelike and interesting, and it is their idiosyncrasies that lead to the several turns in the story. The characters are convincing because they are realistic, not idealized caricatures. In the novel Seth explores the psychological possibilities that shape the behaviour of his characters in a convincing and realistic manner. John's petulant rashness is a logical by-product of his unhappy childhood, as Janet's and Liz's tolerance stems from their solid family structure. The neuroticism that each character exhibits, to a lesser or greater extent, is the regrettable legacy of unrelenting pressure to perform better in every walk of life. Each character that appears before the reader is easy to place in real-life California. One recognizes that countless John's exist, trapped not only in Silicon Valley, which Seth calls "ambition's ulcer alley" (7), but wherever there is an overemphasis on materialistic goals. The portrayal of homosexuality is very realistic too. The psychological and social dilemmas that homosexuals face are admirably portrayed by Seth, each point of view receiving his equal attention and rhetoric. Seth seems to have drawn the characters, even their dialogue, from direct contact with life, and coupled this with a knack for psychoanalysis that Freud himself might have envied.

Nature also receives her due share of attention in the novel. Seth's poetic fancy cannot help but notice each blossoming shrub, each swathe of colour in Nature's autumn finery, the slow march of the seasons, the biannual migration of the birds and whales, the way even the hills change colour from dawn to dusk. Nature is an inseparable part of the world Seth's characters inhabit and impresses herself upon their sensibilities almost compellingly. To illustrate:

[...] The crisp features of the season:
The straw-gold hill, this oak-strewn place,
With here the flutter of a dusty
Sparrow, and there the encroaching rusty
Lichen upon the rock where Paul
Sits singing to himself, and all
The hillsides burred with skeletal thistles
And thorn brush, and the clear cool air
Presaging winter rain, and there
A mockingbird with chacks and whistles
Liquidly aviating through
A sky of Californian blue [...] (55).

Seth does not use nature to contrast the beauty and simplicity of the Natural world with the sordidness and complexity of human life, but to the characters in the novel, the apprehension of natural phenomena brings them a serenity that is absent in their lives. It is for this reason that Janet, in spite of the busy life she leads, goes to the bay to watch the whales migrate south for the winter; John, though cynical and worldly-wise, is not immune to the beauty of the hills.

The Golden Gate is, thus, in the words of A.N. Kaul, "an extraordinary book about ordinary life."[11] It has been hailed as the great Californian novel, because the themes it treats of: disillusionment from love, estrangement, discontentment at the work place, silicon Valley, nuclear bombs, one night stands, homosexuality, rock music—all these coalesce into a very detailed picture of life in the coastal, cosmopolitan city of San Francisco, which represents the entire state of California in miniature. But in spite of the local topography that Seth introduces: the golden gate bridge, fisherman's wharf, and the bay area and so on, the story could be about any given set of people anywhere in the world, and their concurrent modes of existence. The subject matter of the novel is not for one particular place but for all places and for all time: love, life, work, eating, drinking, politics, conversation, music, parties, friendship, alienation, death, birth, loneliness, pain. These are the issues addressed, and by embracing these universal vistas, Seth makes the novel much more than just a novel about life in an American city. But again, there is nothing here that California does not possess. This is because of Seth's total involvement with California. Seth emphasizes that it was not his detachment but his love of California that was most valuable to him in the writing of this novel. Leslie quotes Seth, who says:

> One can't come with a cold and objective eye from outside and then write with affection about a place. One must have lived in that place and not just observed for years.[12]

The novel is thus plush with details about California. Seth paints the city of San Francisco in all its colourful glory, delineating all the minute things that constitute the heartbeat of the city: pumpkin pie, bubble gum, freeways, traffic cops chasing speeding cars, witty bumper stickers, billboards, demonstrations, the bay area, the gay bars; the city is presented as a living, pulsating entity in which intellectual progress co-exists with sexual licentiousness. This is done specifically to highlight the superficiality of man's existence in such a city, where life has degenerated into an endless striving with no meaning. Even the language is reproduced as it is spoken; it is replete with the colour and idiom of American English. Thus, both linguistically and thematically, the novel is an American novel. The picture of San Francisco that Seth conjures up is three dimensional. From the way the mind of the city works, its physical attributes, its oddities, its moral standards, work ethics, single parenting, love, leisure, friendship, altogether create quite a complete mosaic. Seth says that it was during his years in America that he learned how to have fun. He says, "I loved the sunshine [...] the freedom, the sense of ease in the personalities."[13] This joie de vivre is distilled into *The Golden Gate*, the reason that for all its tragedy, it is not a depressing novel.

Yet, the novel is more than just a realistic look at California in all its hedonistic glee. It is a gentle and urbane satire upon life in a fast paced culture. By focusing on the improbable probability of a nuclear holocaust, Seth enlarges the scope of the novel. The story becomes serious and moves beyond the personal concerns of the characters. In this section

Seth speaks as "a citizen of the world, neither with specific accusations nor with solutions, but with concern."[14]

Seth also takes a close look at the institution of marriage. The ideal marriages presented in the novel are those of Janet's parents and Liz's parents. Both these marriages are based on old world values, with both spouses committed to one another and to their respective families. In stark contrast is the marriage of Phil with Claire and the relationship between John and Liz. Both these associations falter because they have been made by people who are too self-involved to try to change themselves for someone else. On the other hand, Phil and Liz succeed in maintaining a relationship chiefly because they have learnt a lesson from their previous relationships. Seth also advocates that shared likes and dislikes and compatible interests, not mere physical attraction, are the foundations of a long term relationship. Liz ultimately recognizes this and it is for this reason that she chooses the dull but sensible Phil over the passionate but volatile John and Seth seems to commend her choice.

The novel becomes a bildungsroman as it traces the growth of John from his childish, petulant phase to a maturity and an acceptance of life. The novel both begins and ends with John alone, but in the course of the tale John comes some way towards understanding and tolerance, recognizing the value of such mundane institutions as friendship and marriage. The bildungsroman thus maps the journey of John from stumbling blindness to self discovery. Seth makes all the characters, and most of all John, recognize that money, power, or any such worldly standards must not become ends in themselves.

That *The Golden Gate* is a striking achievement and that in it Seth has mastered the creative art process is indisputable. Also, his mastery of style and diction cannot go unnoticed. The verse seems to flow effortlessly. Whether it is description or conversation or even mental reflection Seth harnesses the sonnet to fashion a tale that never lapses into boredom. Seth's diction is interspersed with Latin and French influences and displays his inarguable but non-overbearing scholarship. The sparse restrained style is combined with a character driven narrative, spiced with urbane satire, and all is wrapped in humour tempered with compassion that bathes the entire work in a gentle light. Seth maintains the pace of the novel throughout, only varying the tone in some places in order to avoid monotony. His tone is lightly ironic and witty, and he has that ability of the true artist to see the world around him very perceptively. As the drama unfolds, with its naïve joys, blind rage, then sudden tragedy, it reflects on the wider issues afflicting mankind, the place of love in human life, and the sacrifices required before one is entitled to the happiness that love brings.

The unabated popularity of the novel is not due merely to the novelty of its expression—it is in large measure due to the novelty of its telling—the easy, narrative, camaraderial style, the ready admittance and justification of using an obsolete form, the sartorial wit, the easy elegance that permeates the descriptions of even the most mundane turn of events, the feeling that here is an author who is truly of one's time and yet elevated above it due to his faculty of perceptive farsightedness. He tells a tale of human weakness and failing, and expresses urgent concern about mankind's headlong rush towards collective doom, jolting the reader out of his complacency, forcing him to sit up and think; to establish where his priorities lie, as an individual, and in a broader context, as a citizen of the world.

The novel was awarded the 1986 British Airways Commonwealth Poetry Prize.

Notes

1. Pushkin, *Eugene Onegin*.
2. *The Golden Gate*, Random House Inc. New York, 1986, 101.
3. Diana Trilling, "The Inage of Women in Contemporary Literature," *The Woman in America*, ed. R.J. Litton, Boston, Houghton Mifflin, 1965, 61.
4. A. Towne, *Homosexuality in American Culture*, American Mercury, August 1951, LXXIII, 3-9
5. Alan Hollinghurst, "In The Onegin Line," the *Times Literary Supplement*, July 4, 1986.
6. Byron, *Don Juan*.

7. A.N. Kaul, "Wise and Witty," *Indian Literature*—Sahitya Academy Bimonthly no.132, July-August, 1989, 106.
8. Katherine Knorr, "Vikram Seth Plays to His Truest Judges." *International Herald Tribune* Online Edition. Apr 24, 1999.
9. S. Karunakaran, "Games the Novelists Play," *Fiction of the Nineties*, ed. U.V. Das and R.K. Dhawan, Prestige Books, 1994, 94.
10. Karunakaran, *loc cit.*
11. Kaul, *loc cit.*
12. Leslie Jacques, "Rhyme and Reason," *Span*, Nov. 1986.
13. Jeremy Gavron, "A Suitable Joy," *Daily Mail* and *Guardian*, July 20, 1999.
14. Ruth Morse, *Rooted Cosmopolite: Vikram Seth And 'The Scars of Middlemarch.'* Fitzwilliam College, Cambridge. URL:www.perso.worldonline.fr/ebc/s.html.c. cit.

4

Vikram Seth's Literary Mammoth: *A Suitable Boy*

A Suitable Boy, for many reasons, has been perceived as Seth's chef-d'oeuvre, his "three and a half pounds of perfection,"[1] as Jonathan Yardley so aptly put it. But that is merely the tip of the iceberg. Literary merit aside, *A Suitable Boy* is a landmark in Seth's career because it represents a sort of coming-of-age, Seth's formal donning of the mantle of a writer. The novel also grounds him for the first time, in Indian soil. First, because although Seth's travelogue *From Heaven Lake* is also written from the point of view of an Indian sensibility, in it Seth does not refer to India except occasionally and that too only in a demographic context. It is with *A Suitable Boy* that Seth focuses on India, an India that furnishes him with a muse, and a rather weighty one at that.

Seth calls Mrs. Rupa Mehra (a character in the novel), "the muse of the project. She arrived one day and said, 'This is the story of me and my daughters.'"[2]

But what started out as a simple tale involving a small cast of characters gradually grew into the sprawling canvas of *A Suitable Boy*, ostensibly seeking to put an entire sub-continent between its covers. Seth explains how this came about, saying that he wanted to write about India and planned to write a series of five short novels. Instead, he wrote one rather long novel about India of the 1950s. Seth had planned that he would deal swiftly with this period and then go forward to the

Sino-Indian war, the Emergency etc., but he got stuck in that period. The more he researched it, the more the topics obsessed him—Zamindari abolition, courtesans losing their sources of income, the British having left, the new kind of politicians moving in.[3] Consequently, what Seth had envisioned would be his two square inches of ivory, gradually broadened, first into a Victorian oil painting, and then even beyond that into an embroidered and patched American quilt, "embellished by that multiplicity of detail that gives it density and richness."[4] Not surprisingly, for all its length, the novel turned out to be that rarity: a literary bestseller.

The novel opens in 1952 with Mrs. Rupa Mehra's words to her younger daughter Lata, on her elder daughter's wedding day: "You, too, will marry a boy I choose."[5] The very words imply an uneasy feeling that maternal authority needs to be exercised over Lata, who might be harbouring revolutionary ideas of her own. These words also establish the *status quo* of the structure of Indian society, where it is the parents who choose brides and grooms for their children. Lata and Savita (Lata's elder sister) are two sides of the same coin of Indian womanhood. Savita is the epitome of the duty-bound, culturally traditional girl, whereas Lata represents the changing persona of the Indian woman—her first tentative steps towards broader horizons in free India.

Behind this search for a suitable boy for Lata are four parallel stories, encompassing four families: the Mehras, the Kapoors, the Chatterjees, and the Khans, all skeins in a canvas on which is woven an intricate story, as complex as India itself. Together these families furnish the social structure of post-independence India. Connected by either marriage or friendship, these four families cleverly balance a saga of social manners with a historical account of the Indian sub-continent trying its fledgling wings amidst the chaos of politics, religion, language, the land reform movement and so on.

The narrative is bracketed by two weddings and in between, Seth 'creates a world,' to borrow a term usually reserved for Jane Austen. The sheer breadth of the novel encompasses on the one hand, parliamentary speeches, the trauma of partition, the Zamindari abolition bill, communal tensions, the flavour of India's first general election—to the scandalously modern lifestyle of upper-crust Calcutta, University life, the fading world of ghazals and courtesans and old-world courtesy, and the comic world of the Chatterjees and Mrs. Rupa Mehra on the other. To the Mehras and the Chatterjees falls the light comedy, while the Kapoors and the Khans furnish the drama.

Displaying his genius at story-telling, Seth grounds his narrative in some of the most important social and political issues of the day. The Khans are Muslim Zamindars, whose ancient feudal fiefs are in danger of being taken away if the land reform bill is passed. The Kapoors have as their patriarch a powerful minister of revenue, who is also a member of the National Legislative Assembly. The Chatterjees are Brahmos and have the first Indian High Court Justice as their patriarch; the Mehras boast one of the first Indian "brown-sahibs," executives in high-profile British management firms.

However, despite the grand scale on which the novel is conceived, Seth's focus is not primarily on these issues. The main interest lies in the search for a suitable boy, and in the portrayal of family dramas. Robert Worth states, "Seth appears bent on showing us the interstices of social change, the way life will go on, no matter what history may be up to."[6] *A Suitable Boy* thus explores many aspects of Indian life: arranged marriage, independence, love, family, prostitution, politics, poverty, culture, and individualism—all under the garb of a gently-paced tale of social manners.

The writing of *A Suitable Boy* is as much a labour of love for its author as it a joy of readership for its readers. However, it would be incorrect to assume that in writing *A Suitable Boy*, Seth is pandering to the West's preconceived and clichéd notions of the East, presenting his Western readership with what it eagerly savours: India's mysticism, strange customs and colourful culture. Also, his treatment of this theme could not be more different than that of previous Indian writers who have written about India. Mulk Raj Anand's *The Private Life of an Indian Prince*[7] and Manohar Malgaonkars *The Princes*[8] are two well-known attempts to deal with the issue of the Land Reform Bill, entailing the merger of the princely states into the Indian union. But Seth's novel is different: it is political only in the sense that action, character, and setting of a certain set of characters are more or less grounded in politics in it. The political material is properly integrated with the fictional content of the work. In this respect, Seth is most unlike these nationalistic writers who are so pre-occupied with their memories and angst that they make their novels tools to voice their dissent. The only Indian writer Seth can be compared to is R.K. Narayan who also focuses on the story and how best to tell it, rather than on his sense of Indianness. For Seth, India has provided him with the inspiration to create an engaging work of art: it has not orbited him into a search for his Indian roots and his novel does not serve as a vehicle to launch a diatribe against colonialism. The contrast is evident especially because the period the novel deals with is fertile ground for expressing the covert nationalism that is so typical of the post-colonial novel and from which Seth abstains. Seth does not mean *A Suitable Boy* to be the Great Indian Novel. It is to this freedom from tenseness that *A Suitable Boy* owes its light touch and it is for this reason that reading it is far from the potentially monolithic task it might seem to be.

Comparison with Salman Rushdie's *Midnight's Children*[9] becomes inevitable due to the stark contrast in treatment of the same theme: post-independence India as the subject and Indian family life as its vehicle. Rushdie's novel is quite in character with his other work: feverish, opinionated, and overwhelming. Seth's view is serene, cultured, concerned, and balanced. Rushdie focuses on elements that tear society apart, while Seth focuses on the ones that bring society together, thereby aiming at a comprehensive unity of vision. *A Suitable Boy* thus displays Seth's social conscience in its firm renunciation of anti-secularism and corruption, one of the book's themes being religious intolerance. Seth says about this aspect of the novel, "Clearly my book is partly a plea for tolerance. I wish these loonies (religious fanatics) would allow ordinary people to get on with their ordinary lives."[10]

The two main themes are the elusive search for love, and religious intolerance. Regarding the former, it is not difficult to appreciate the dilemma of Mrs. Rupa Mehra regarding Kabir as an unsuitable boy, in the aftermath of partition. Far from the orderly exchange envisioned by the British, the communal bloodshed that ensued is an experience that few who lived through it can ever forget. Seth describes India's community-oriented society with surprising objectivity, consistently maintaining a secular tone, even while describing religious rites, processions and beliefs. But he does not downplay the "tragic interweaving of religion and politics, the ancient rivalry between Hindu and Muslim, the undying suspicion and resentment that can be blown into flame at any moment by unscrupulous office seekers or bigoted religious leaders."[11] In all these respects, Seth does not gild the lily and his portrayal of the India of the 1950s holds true even today, because so much in India remains unchanged. Regarding the quest for love, Seth holds fast to his earlier philosophy (as evinced in *The Golden Gate*), seemingly advocating that a level headed commitment is more enduring than youth's dreams of passion. *A Suitable Boy* presents its characters with many choices—most of them dark and heavy. Maan has to choose between Saeeda Bai and his father's reputation, Lata has to choose between the first love of her life (Kabir) and her mother's happiness. The novel presents passion gone awry, and Seth emphasizes that the search should be not for love but for life-mate. Seth does not believe that passion always goes wrong. He says that, "it's just that in the circumstances of my particular characters, things didn't work out; but that's no reason why they shouldn't, given a different set of people and circumstances."[12] Yet, his plot resolutions seem to indicate otherwise, and he also agrees: "there are other things (besides true love), and they do impinge upon people. I can't take the view that you can live on love and fresh air."[13] Consequently, *A Suitable Boy* is about much more than a girl choosing a suitable husband. It is an exploration of all the trials that must be endured before enough strength has been acquired to do the right thing. Rational calm must prevail over tumultuous passion, the mind must exercise restraint upon the libido, and passion must become subservient to plain common sense. In her somewhat dramatic renunciation of love, Lata firmly turns her back on romance, having come to the realization that romance is all very well, but a good marriage requires a stability that comes from shared customs and beliefs. Lata does not reject Kabir solely because her mother disapproves—but she becomes more sympathetic to her mother's point of view and starts to see Kabir in a new light once she realises that he is not willing to just carry her off into the sunset. It is unfortunate that she falls in love with the wrong man, but that is just one of the ironies of life. Her ultimately opting for Haresh is the sanest decision she has ever made—not at her mother's behest or her brother's, but as an independent decision. She knows that Haresh does not meet her brother Arun's snobbish standards and neither is her mother really sure that he will be able to keep Lata happy, yet she chooses him because she perceives in Haresh's sincerity a quality that she instinctively finds extremely appealing for a stable married life. For Lata, marriage entails stability and prosperity, and she accepts that she cannot jeopardize these goals for the sake of an attachment that even she recognizes is little more than a romantic vision.

Maan's infatuation with Saeeda Bai is also an aberration, for which he must ultimately pay the price. Maan's entire life is slightly out of kilter, in sharp contrast to his brother's intellectuality and his father's idealism. He is a wastrel and although he does have an innate goodness, the weakness of his character proves to be his undoing. He has been given the role of the conventional un-heroic hero who even has a homosexual relationship with his friend Firoz, although it is ultimately subsidiary to heterosexual marriage impulses. After the stabbing of Firoz and his father's defeat in the election (chiefly on account of Maan's notoriety) he finally come to his senses and renounces passion, albeit more dramatically than Lata does. He, too, chooses family over passion, good sense over sensuality, and is shown to be the better for it. In both cases (Lata's and Maan's), the implied reading is that as thinking, rational beings, one has an obligation to make the correct choices if there is to be a sense of order in the society one creates. Lata could just as easily have chosen Kabir—and become estranged from her mother and her entire cultural moorings, and Maan could have continued his sad little liaison with an ageing courtesan and let his life slip through his fingers in the process —but Seth cares too much about his characters to allow them to do that. The choices each one makes are difficult but they must be made and there is no use moping about what could have been. This is the world of love that Seth creates—a world not clouded by unrealistic dreams, and firmly entrenched in the reality of life.

As regards style, it becomes evident that *A Suitable Boy* has been written with the leisureliness, the almost forgotten confidence of the Victorian novel. It is a throwback to an earlier generation when the art of novel-writing was an extension of raconteuring. Seth dons the mantle of omniscient author, but the authorial voice in *A Suitable Boy* is never conspicuous or overbearing. The novel is written with the quiet and unobtrusive style which Seth attributes to his own tastes and beliefs.

In this novel Seth's displays a taste for scrupulous documentation. As a result, each major setting in the novel—the weddings of Lata and Savita, the pul-mela, the raising of the Shiva-lingam, the religious festivities—is elaborately reproduced in its social and demographic entirety. Seth is in no hurry to wind up his saga and his unerring eye for detail leaves out nothing - he is not content merely with a page or two long description of Saeeda Bai sing—he must take the reader through the entire evening couplet by couplet, ghazal by ghazal. Every nuance, every gesture ("ada") is perfectly caught. For this reason *A Suitable Boy* can be a little hard on those readers who prefer fast paced novels. It is a novel strictly for those who are willing to be drawn, albeit temporarily, into the world that Seth creates.

Seth's use of language in the novel is also unique, because *A Suitable Boy* is the only work in Seth's canon that occasions an examination of language. All Seth's other works employ flawless English, but with such an Indian subject, a tale written in unadulterated English would perhaps not have been so convincing, apart from being less apposite as well. India has adopted the English language for her own, blending it with every local dialect, so that it is no longer spoken as the Queen's English except by the élite. Consequently, the Indianisms in *A Suitable Boy* are confined to middle class society. In such instances it becomes clear that the language being spoken is not English but Urdu, Hindi, or even Bengali, and Seth has provided a literal translation in order to preserve the idiom, without which the entire conversation would be lost. This gives rise to quaint expressions like, "they want to suck my blood," (1099) "illumine our Gathering" (1099), "my this" (177), (for husband), to pinpoint a few. This use of language affects a great deal of verisimilitude in the novel and enables Seth to delineate characters and their mindsets effectively. In the context of language it is noteworthy that Seth's passion for versification spills over into *A Suitable Boy*, with the academic connection through Pran and Lata, the weekly poetry sessions of the Brahmapur Literary Society, Amit's vocation, and the Chatterjee family's natural facility with silly rhyme providing Seth with many opportunities to indulge himself.

Seth's style is so unique that the reader is irresistibly held by Seth's narrative technique, which is never heavy or dull, even when he is describing the drudgeries of Indian politics. The literary tradition Seth has inherited is essentially Western, and so the Russian literary model adds *War and Peace* to *Eugene Onegin* and blends it with the Victorian model named in the novel itself—*Middlemarch*. Literary allusions are employed from Austen, Flaubert, E.M. Forrester, and like Eliot, Seth's use of pastiche enables him to intensify the character delineation. Critics have zealously compared Seth's style to Jane Austen's and there is little doubt that Seth does seem to share some of Austen's artistic goals, among them the desire to portray ordinary people living ordinary lives. In *A Suitable Boy* too, marriage is central to the theme, but unlike Austen's precise craftsmanship, this central theme is but one of several. Seth shares Austen's level headed approach towards marriage, reiterating that plain common sense should govern one's actions rather than romantic visions, although a fusion of the two would be ideal. Seth also shares with Austen an innate conservatism evident in his insistence on a natural world order, a restoration of the golden mean so to speak, as the key to salvation. Like Austen, Seth too finds suffering unpleasant, and like her, his personal reaction in the novel is reduced to a minimum. But these similarities must end here, for Seth has a trademark style of his own, distilled out of his eclectic reading and moulded by his own personality. It would be fruitless to compare his style with Tolstoy's brooding meditations or with Austen's sharp irony. Likewise, though ostentatiously modelled on *Middlemarch*, *A Suitable Boy* shares none of George Eliot's zeal for reform. Like Chaucer, Seth's keen eye notices each foible, each aberration, but he believes that he is no one to set the crooked straight. In addition, he is too tolerant and too fond of his characters to want to transform them.

Seth's style in this novel involves conjuring up a brilliant sense of the comic, evident especially when he writes about the Chatterjees and their circle. The overwhelming atmosphere of the novel is one of tongue-in-cheek humour, despite the occasional dark storm clouds that gather. It is as if Seth is exhorting the reader to dwell on the comic aspects of everyday life rather than on the tragic ones, aware that reducing one's problems to the playful silliness of Kakoli-couplets will rob them of some of their gravity. Seth also seeks to divest the Indian Holy men and gurus of their mystic spirituality, presenting them as the majority of them really are—opportunists. The swamis and the gullibility of their devotees provide some highly comic scenes in the novel. Yet, the happy spirit of the novel is neither sentiment nor blind, "it is a natural gift of the author, who never mocks or dismisses his characters."[14] Consequently, Seth's voice is not the voice of indignation but that of gentle and genteel comedy.

A noteworthy feature of *A Suitable Boy* is its almost photographic realism. Seth goes to great lengths to procure this effect. From the conversation to the landscaping, from the rich splendour of Saeeda Bai's chambers to the rustic simplicity of Rasheed's household, from the Chatterjee mansion to Mrs. Rupa Mehra's annual rail pilgrimage, there is no doubt whatsoever in the reader's mind that things are exactly as Seth portrays them. Seth takes great pleasure in describing what he sees, and he has the knack to see straight to salient feature, or conversely, to its absurdity. The writing of such a book requires a keen sense of life—a resource far more powerful then even technical skill—and Seth's writing displays no dearth of both. Much of the realism in the novel is achieved by dint of Seth's exhaustive research of that period. After Seth began writing the novel, he came to a dead stop and concentrated on research for about a year, burying himself in old newspapers, accounts of legislative debates, interviewing people from that era, even the owner of a dog named Cuddles about the people Cuddles had bitten. He spent weeks living in a village in rural U.P. and with leather workers in Agra, and talked to musicians, judges, even owners of parrots. Seth thus relied heavily on the historical material of the period and fashioned a tale that endeavours to include every major facet of the multi-faceted Indian reality.

Seth is able to convince the reader of his historical accuracy by the painstaking reproduction of the politics of the time. The state of Poorva Pradesh is clearly Eastern U.P. and the city of Brahmapur is a coalition of Lucknow, Agra, and Allahabad. It may not be coincidence that Brahmapur and Allahabad have the same literal meaning. The political personages who played important roles after independence are transformed into their fictional counterparts. Nehru appears as himself, while Pandit S.S. Sharma, the first chief minister of Poorva Pradesh is clearly Pandit Govind Vallabh Pant. Mahesh Kapoor, the revenue minister, and L.N. Aggarwal, home minister in the Sharma ministry are Chandrabhan Gupta and Dr. Sampoornanda respectively, with their parallel political rivalry. All these characters firmly anchor the novel in the politics of the period. Seth's treatment of this political theme is like his treatment of every other—laid back, analytical, and accurate. He pays great attention to the land-reform bill, which once passed in parliament, was to affect far-reaching changes; his training in Economics enables him to analyze the economics of village life and the system of a local currency based on chits.

The social realism in the novel is equally convincing. Calcutta is an apt choice for the setting of a cosmopolitan family like the Chatterjees, as Calcutta was the social, cultural, and political capital of the British in those days, long before Delhi became the centre of things. The Chatterjees are anglicized upper middle class Bengalis, and Brahmos to boot. Brahmoism was founded by Raja Ram Mohan Roy and postulated the Upanishidic message that God is one, though called by different names. Brahmoism thus has an intellectual appeal and a refined spirituality. By making the Chatterjees Brahmos, Seth is able to establish their non-conservatism. Shyam S. Agarwal writes, "It is but natural that Seth, writing on the intellectual minority in India in 1951-52, should choose Calcutta, like Tolstoy, who chose St. Petersburg for War and Peace."[15]

The Chatterjee children, with their different eccentricities, are extensions of this theme of social realism. As is common in Calcutta among the idle rich, "none of them worked, but each had an occupation." (383) Amit, despite having studied law at Oxford, was quite content in his role as a dreamy poet; Dipanker was equally qualified but preferred to ponder the meaning of life from the sanctuary of his room; Meenakshi had lost her cultural moorings—she played canasta and indulged in extra-marital escapades; Kakoli monopolized the phone, and Tapan, who studied at school, was yet too small to develop his own way of occupying himself without actually doing anything. In this context it is noteworthy that in the delineation of the Chatterjees, there is not the slightest hint of censure or even of sarcasm, although Seth does use them to furnish much of the social comedy.

Along with the Chatterjees, the parallel world of Brahmapur and Saeeda Bai entices the reader into a fast fading era that will soon become history. Seth re-creates India of the 1950s for the reader piece by piece, reproducing University academics with its rampant political rivalries and its dead end stagnation, the world of Mrs. Rupa Mehra, with all her manoeuvrings to find a suitable son-in-law, religious zealots who perpetrate riots, or scheming politicians who aid them—especially the episode about the raising of the Shiva Lingam on the disputed site—all become relevant in light of the Ayodhya episode and the recent Gujarat violence. Seth brings the reader into the homes of the people who bear the impact of this religious frenzy. As the novel progresses, every aspect of Indian society is explored. Ruth Morse states:

> It is striking that Seth should locate the problems that plague the subcontinent in India's own development, not only from such an early period, because there is a strident tendency in modern Indian life to blame all such corruptions upon the legacy of the Raj.[16]

The reality that Seth presents is neither exaggerated nor unreal. Seth shows India as she is, warts and all, not the holier-than-thou pictures that earlier writers favoured. This is a land where communal insanity can flare up at the drop of a hat, a land where morals and spirituality have been lost somewhere on the road to self-advancement, and a land where corruption is so rampant that it has become a way of life. Agarwalla states:

> Seth shows the "India of withering idealism, rotting corruption, pestering communal disharmony, parasitical intrigue of politicians, the perpetual fight between the forces of progress and modernity and the forces of tradition and obscurism."[17]

Seth's style, thus, incorporates all the aforementioned features into it, resulting in the technical virtuosity that enables him to write such a long, complex novel.

In the grand sprawl of *A Suitable Boy*, the narrative tension that drives a more compact novel is perhaps inevitably lost. Yet, despite all the digressions and seemingly irrelevant subplots, *A Suitable Boy* possesses formal logic, and it steadily progresses towards the finale, when the search for a suitable boy is finally over. The main plot—the search for the perfect groom, carries with it all the subplots in an even handed and artistically linked fashion. Seth says about the plot of *A Suitable Boy*, "This novel is linear partly because it is multi linear. There are several plots in it,"[18] and they help the main plot to stand on a firmer footing. Some of the plots look expendable at first glance but are actually vehicles for Seth's meditations on life: the art of learning one's craft and the way a craft is constructed, and Seth's insights, usually very perceptive, on human nature. Representing, like *Middlemarch*, the society of a generation ago, Seth effortlessly rustles up a variety of plots to take on India on the eve of her first general election, stopping to focus on every issue that might conceivably have a bearing on it. In the words of Ruth Morse, "*A Suitable Boy* is social satire and social history, from the politics of the great man to the manoeuvrings of a mother."[19] The central plot, the matrimonial quest of Mrs. Rupa Mehra, is thus intertwined with the quest of all the other characters in their different ways.

The vast expanse of the novel does not leave Seth with much time to develop his characters. For the most part, the characters in the novel are conventionally drawn, and "come to us extremely well equipped with easily recognizable characteristics."[20] At the end of the novel they have not grown, with the exception of Maan and Lata. But what saves them from banality is Seth's according them with details and traits that ring true. From the Mehras to the Chatterjees, from the Khans to the Kapoors, these characters are drawn from real life, and though the reader is privy only to part of their personalities, the parts portrayed are recognizable as real. Seth does not explore his characters to their full potential, not staying with any character long enough to render the character unforgettable. His chief interest lies in the narrative. It is for this reason that *A Suitable Boy* works more as an extremely interesting period documentary than as a novel. Yet, it is hard to disagree with Nilanjana S. Roy who says, "with all its flaws, *A Suitable Boy* is more captivating than more technically perfect novels that followed in its wake for it offers that most old fashioned of all qualities—charm."[21]

In this novel, family, and family relationships resume centre stage, as they once did in the nineteenth century realistic novel. Seth's handling of the institution of marriage is generous and uncynical, and there are little of the darker aspects of Indian married life—dowry, and bride-burning, for instance—yet never for a moment does the novel seem to be contrived. Seth's clear, straightforward style represents an attempt to let his characters and their world stand free from authorial intrusion. With his respect for family values, Seth binds scores of characters in strands of marriage and friendship.

Seth thus seeks to interpret the Victorian tradition of novel writing in an Indian context, and the result is a striking achievement, with its Victorian demands upon the reader and its conscientious seriousness about public life. The pages of *A Suitable Boy* brim with a quiet praise for ordinary life. Great storytellers have no need to sensationalize. They simply present, and, by the force of their clarity and empathy, keep the reader's unflagging interest. This is Seth's indisputable achievement in this novel.

It is perhaps for this reason that in spite of the novel's wrist-spraining and purse-straining drawbacks, it has drawn world wide acclaim. Seth says that when the novel would show no signs of winding up, he would often tell himself, "There must be an audience for a tale cleanly told—no matter how long it is."[22] He was right, because in *A Suitable Boy*, he has created a world that will entice readers for decades to come.

A Suitable Boy won the W.H. Smith Connect award in 1993.

Notes

1. Jonathan Yardley, "A Dickens for the Subcontinent," the *Washington Post*, 25 April, 1993.
2. John Bemrose, "Full-lotus Fiction—*A Suitable Boy* by Vikram Seth," MacLean Hunter Consumer Publications, Toronto, May 31, 1993.
3. Interview with Amit Roy, the Telegraph (Calcutta), 29 August, 1992.
4. Anita Desai, "Sitting Pretty," the *New York Review* of Books. May 27, 1993.
5. *A Suitable Boy*, Viking Penguin India Ltd. 1993, 3

6. Robert Worth, "India—All of it—*A Suitable Boy*," *Commonwealth Foundation*, May 21, 1993.
7. Mulk Raj Anand, *The Private Life of an Indian Prince*, London, Hutchinson, 1963.
8. Manohar Malgaonkar, *The Princes*, Orient Paperbacks, New Delhi, 1963.
9. Salman Rushdie, *Midnight's Children*, Penguin, USA, 1991.
10. Eugene Robinson, "A Tolstoy—On his First Try," *Washington Post*, May 1, 1993.
11. Robert Towers, "Good Enough for Her Mother's Mother's Mother," *New York Times*, May 9, 1993.
12. *Rediff Interview*, "The Vikram Seth Chat." URL: www.rediff.com/chat/vikcha.html
13. *Ibid.*
14. Bemrose, *loc cit.*
15. Shyam S. Agarwalla, *Vikram Seth's A Suitable Boy—Search for an Indian Identity*, Prestige Books, 1995, 53.
16. Ruth Morse, *Rooted Cosmopolite: Vikram Seth and 'The Scars of Middlemarch.'* Fitzwilliam College, Cambridge. URL:www.perso.worldonline.fr/ebc/s.html
17. Agarwalla, *ibid.*
18. Interview with Seema Paul, the *Telegraph Magazine*, Feb. 21, 1993, 9.
19. Morse, *loc cit.*
20. Desai, *loc cit.*
21. Nilanjana S. Roy, "The secret of Being a Bore is to Say Everything," URL:www.indiawrites.com/archives.cfm?
22. Bemrose, *loc cit.*

5

An Equal Music: An Offering from the Heart

An Equal Music was conceived one wintry day in London, while Seth was taking a walk in Hyde Park with his friend Philippe Honoré. Seth recalls that as they were walking, he saw in his mind's eye a tallish figure, European or American by race, dressed against the weather. This person was looking intently at the water of the lake in the park. Inexplicably fascinated by him, Seth turned to his friend and told him that he had a feeling that this imaginary person had something to do with his next book, and wondered as to what his profession was, what was making him look so pensively at the waters of the lake, and other such questions. Then Honoré, who is a musician, decided that this person was a musician too. That's how the novel began. The muse here was thus this imaginary, ordinary person staring intently at the water. As Seth says, "It's a very visual inspiration for a very aural novel."[1]

Published in 1999, *An Equal Music* belongs characteristically in Seth's repertoire by virtue of it being stunningly different from all his previous work. All Seth's books are one-offs and this one is no different. The backdrop of the novel is the enchanted, romantic world of Vienna and Venice, and the subject is Western Europe's supreme cultural achievement: classical music.

In several ways, *An Equal Music* presents a kind of antithesis to *A Suitable Boy*. It is everything that *A Suitable Boy* is not. In the latter, Seth articulates life from a distance, hurrying over all that he considers even remotely distasteful, firmly shunning any intense emotions. As a result, *A Suitable Boy* resonates with a gentle, laid-back serenity. By contrast, *An Equal Music* takes a determined look at the darker passions—unhappiness, obsession, and addresses difficult issues about love and life in the process. Again, unlike the sprawling canvas of *A Suitable Boy, An Equal Music* limits its scope to the professional and private world of a musician and the cities of London, Venice and Vienna. Also, *An Equal Music* is a love story, not a romantic saga like *A Suitable Boy* was. It is deeper and more serious, portraying the kind of love that can survive even decade-long separations. On another level this is a story that explores the strangely obsessive and neurotic life that a professional musician leads.

The book has been written in the first person. Michael Holme, the narrator, describes himself as "irreparably imprinted with the die of someone else's being."[2] This someone is Julia McNicholl—his fellow music student in Vienna ten years ago and the one true love of his life. Back then in Vienna, both Michael and Julia were passionately devoted to each other and to their music. They found that their music complemented each other's very well and formed a trio with another musician. But owing to an irreconcilable war of wills with their stern teacher, Karl Cäll, Michael, who was nervy and strong headed left Vienna and unintentionally, Julia. By the time he recovered from his distress two months had elapsed, and Julia, hurt beyond redemption, was lost to him forever.

Ten years later, where the novel begins, Michael is earning his living as a second violinist in a string quartet, the Maggiore. Michael spends his days listlessly, with only music providing an emotional anchor and in effect, any meaning to his life. The book's three brief opening paragraphs set the tone of the novel, bringing home to the reader the loneliness that is Michael's lot in life, a loneliness that is only briefly assuaged by long walks and ruminations, a loneliness that clearly attracts Michael to the dark water the wind is blowing at him:

> The branches are bare, the sky tonight a milky violet. It is not quiet here, but it is peaceful. The wind ruffles the black water towards me.
>
> There is no one about. The birds are still. The traffic slashes through Hyde Park. It comes to my ears as white noise.
>
> I test the bench but do not sit down. As yesterday, as the day before, I stand until I have lost my thoughts. I look at the waters of the Serpentine (3).

Michael's loneliness is emphasized in pathos–inducing descriptions in several parts of the book. For instance, when a salesgirl tells Michael that he is a happy man, Michael tells the reader, "I stared at her with such incredulity that she looked down" (4). This isolation is punctuated by accounts of his tormented past, a past which constantly haunts him, making him yearn for answers, for absolution. Into this chaotic world Julia steps in again, inadvertently at first (when Michael spots her on a London bus, but fails to track her down), and purposely later, when she goes backstage after a Maggiore performance at Wigmore Hall. Unable to resist the power of their past they come together again, but this time under the shadow of Julia's marriage and her hearing loss. Yet, for a brief magical time when they escape to Venice, everything seems possible. Ultimately, however, the perfection that they achieve in making music together somehow eludes them in their love.

This story is then a reworking of the Greek legend of Eurydice and Orpheus. In it, Eurydice dies of snakebite on their wedding day. Orpheus, the greatest musician in the world, refuses to accept her death and descends to the underworld, where he sings so persuasively that Hades allows him to take back his bride, only to lose her again due to lingering doubt and weakness. *An Equal Music* reiterates this parable of love lost and almost regained by the power of music, the desperate bid to revive a dead romance against all odds, the subsequent anguish of heartbreak, and the agonies of accepting loss.

Love, however, is not the sole theme. In fact, music usurps love's place as the driving force that pulls the reader along irresistibly, for *An Equal Music* is a meticulously researched, highly allusive text that stuns as one realizes the depth of resources at Seth's command and the faculty of his artistic vision that enables him to render in words what in the authorial note appended to the novel he describes as a trial and a test. In the authorial note Seth has written:

> Music to me is dearer even than speech. When I realized that I would be writing about it, I was gripped with anxiety. Only slowly did I reconcile myself to the thought of it (385).

Seth's anxiety was justifiable, for expressing one art form by the medium of another is by its very definition a challenge. The critic Bernard Holland once wrote, "I am helpless to write about what music is; I can only record the aftershocks it leaves behind."[3] But Seth rises successfully to the challenge. In his famous Norton lectures delivered at Harvard in 1973, composer/conductor Leonard Bernstein sought to establish parallels between the language of music and the syntax of spoken language. In *An Equal Music* Seth similarly endeavours to make comprehensible and accessible to the reader a world in which music is the theme that unites lives. There is some kind of music on every page: it even insinuates itself into the love story, providing the ethereal framework over which the fragile gossamer threads of the love story are woven.

There is no non-sense about Seth when it comes to music. Every musician will gasp at what Seth has been about to discern and express, for his ability to translate the sounds of music into the written word is astounding. In addition, Seth is highly knowledgeable about the great chamber-music classics of the Viennese school. His awe and passion for these classics is evident, and firmly precludes music that is post classical. In this respect, *An Equal Music* has an almost canonical approach to the classical music repertoire.

In antipodal contrast to Salman Rushdie who tackles the same themes of music and love in *The Ground beneath her feet*,[4] Seth does not depict the life of musicians in a fog of bombastic glee and magic realism. His writing is close to the bone: the private and public life of musicians in a quartet. The strains of performance, where virtuosity is a prerequisite, musical whims, moods, preferences, rehearsals, the fragile relations between the members of a chamber music ensemble—whose members are often as antagonistic offstage as they are empathic on it—every detail is minutely and perfectly delineated.

Seth's own empathy for classical music given an irresistible depth of tone to the narrative: "I am the trout the angler, the brook, the observer" (5), he tells us, as he plays Schubert. The passages describing the making of music evoke a trance-like state that can be actually experienced by the reader. As the Maggiore rehearse, vacillating from impatience with each other to musical perfection, Seth deftly notates the joys of collaboration, trust, and creation. Even the technical difficulties encountered by a string quartet in playing certain pieces are explored in depth—as for instance the need to tone down a viola in order to play Bach's *The Art of the Fugue*.

In remarks intended for Goethe, Beethoven once observed:

> Music, verily, is the mediator between intellectual and sensuous life [...]. Tell him to hear my symphonies and he will say that I am right in saying that music is the one incorporeal entrance into the higher world of knowledge which comprehends mankind but which mankind cannot comprehend.[5]

On this premise Seth bases *An Equal Music*, comprehending that writing about an artist is incomplete without exploring the intricacies of his art. In this exploration Seth's genius shines through: in making accessible to the reader the lifelong immersion in and maintenance of a craft that is the foundation of all serious music making. As one character admits, "This morning I suddenly realized how boring musicians are. All our friends are musicians and we aren't interested in anything except music" (14).

Seth uses the four members of the Maggiore to depict how difficult and complicated the life of a dedicated quartet can be. Piers, a member of the quartet, says:

> It's the weirdest thing, a quartet. I don't know what to compare it to. A marriage? a firm? a platoon under fire? A self-regarding, self-destructive priesthood? It has so many different tensions mixed in with is pleasures (199).

The instrument each member plays must be suited to his or her temperament. Thus, Piers, abrasive, demanding, the leader in the group, makes a classic first violinist; Helen, who provides the viola's supporting role, is constantly pouring oil on troubled waters; Billy, genial, brilliant, selfless, eager to please, is the group's cellist, "light and profound: the base of our harmony, the rock on which we rest" (10). Michael, with his tempestuous, temperamental side does well in his role as second violinist. But despite the differences and the idiosyncrasies of its members, the quartet is a family unit, in which not only the actions of a member but even his or her emotional state affect the dynamics of the entire quartet. Michael says:

> But ours is an odd quadripartite marriage [...]. The audiences who listen to us cannot imagine how earnest, how petulant, how accommodating, how wilful is our quest for something beyond ourselves that we imagine with our separate spirits but are compelled to embody together [...]. How are such mechanics, such stops and starts, such facile irreverence transmuted, in spite of ourselves, into musical gold? (14).

Seth provides the answer when he describes the ritual playing of the scale before the quartet commence to play the actual music: "When I play this I release myself into the spirit of the quartet. I become the music of the scale. I mute my will, I free myself" (10). This release from conflicting individualities into a realm of wholeness is what makes the quartet work:

> A strange composite being we are, not ourselves anymore but the Maggiore [...] in front of us 540 unseen beings intent on 549 different webs of sensation and cerebration and emotion, and through us the spirit of someone scribbling away in 1772 with the sharpened feather of a bird (86).

Seth's language of music can convey every minutiae of the art form. The love story pales in comparison. Moving as Julia's meeting with Michael is (after the performance at Wigmore Hall), it cannot compare with the sublimity of the music that has preceded it, particularly of the arresting encore, the first contrapunctus of Bach's *Art of the Fugue*:

> We play in an energized trance [...]. Our synchronous visions merge, and we are one: with each other, with the world, and with that long dispersed being whose force we receive through the shape of annotated vision and the single swift flowing syllable of his name (90).

Such is the kind of blending of description and emotion through which Seth strives to capture the inexpressible essence of music. Like Proust with the Ventevil sonata, Seth finds in the pattern of sounds "an emotional key to our inner being, a well of memory that can be instantly recalled by a chance arrangement of notes."[6]

The characters in the novel are also totally immersed in their separate worlds of music. Michael's world in one in which the presence of long–dead composers is as corporeal as that of the musicians that perform their works: a world in which Michael's relationship with his Carlo Tononi violin is as real to him as is his relationship with the other members of the quartet or even with Julia.

Seth treats the performers' lives as if they were extensions of the miseries and splendours experienced by the composers whose work they seek to express. Playing in Vienna, Michael sees Schubert sitting among the audience, and without it seeming the least bit out of context, slips into Schubert's imagined stream of thought:

> [...] But it was the year I walked to Hayden's grave, it was the year I died and the earth took my syphilis ridden flesh and typhoid ravaged guts many times around the sun before my quintet for strings was heard by human ears (240).

Seth himself is as intensely involved with the music. Schubert is invoked several times in the novel, and Seth says of him, "His songs have such heavenly concision."[7] Elsewhere he says (of Schubert):

> He doesn't make heavy weather of things. If there's sadness it's very clear. Joy and vigour are very clear as well. He had a wonderful melodic sense. He can go through an entire gamut of emotions in a song three or four minutes long.[8]

This kind of empathy with music and musicians is significant because music is at the very heart of *An Equal Music*. David Blake states, "This writer [Seth] is a servant of music, like his creations,"[9] and truly, nothing matters to these possessed creatures but the sublimity with which they scale a Bach or Brahms, the virtuosity with which they "arrive at an understanding of a work that seems to us both true and original, and an expression of which displaces from our minds —and perhaps for a while, from the minds of those who hear us—any versions, however true, however original, played by other hands" (14). Such is Seth's involvement with music. Commendably, most of the scenes and passages connected with music are convincing. Seth gets it consistently and impressively right.

It is true that *An Equal Music* is substantially technical and can therefore be potentially distracting for every non-musically aware reader. However Seth categorically states that he writes primarily for the reader who knows what he is talking about. It is a situation where he gains some readers and loses some with each work. But the wide acclaim both *A Suitable Boy* and *An Equal Music* have received is testimony that despite exploring very specialized worlds, both novels carry the reader along in a general sense.

Technicality aside, *An Equal Music* also takes an in-depth look at the non-glamorous side to music-making. Michael sums it up: "Years of training, long hours, pathetic pay—and being no good for anything else—and having no choice in what you play—you could feel trapped, even if you loved it once" (188). This is compounded with the steady deterioration of a music culture in schools, the presence of music mafia, and in the case of a quartet or an ensemble of a similar nature, "the proximity to each other and only to each other, which, more often than we recognize, constrict our spirits and makers us stranger than we are. Perhaps even our states of exaltation are akin to the dizziness that comes form lacking air" (76).

In essence, music is what the novel chiefly addresses itself to and those who have been caught in the spell of music will note with widening eyes that Seth is able to call an extraordinary amount of that experience to the page.

The music and the love complement each other remarkably well. The delicate unfurling of the relationship between Michael and Julia is bathed in the glow of musical reference to Mozart, Beethoven, Schubert, and Bach—virtually all the great masters—because their love has their music making as its foundation, their music serving as a metaphor, and possibly as a substitute for their love. For the two principals—Michael and Julia, music is not merely a vocation, it is their avocation, and it has the strength to tie them to each other beyond the boundaries dictated by socially acceptable norms. For Michael, Julia is not only the love of a lifetime—she is the very essence of his craft. The pieces he associates with her he has never been able to perform after Vienna. This is the reason that the chance discovery of Beethoven's string quintet in C major is a dream come true, for Michael knows that unlike with the original trio arrangement, "nothing will seize me up or paralyze my heart or arm" (38).

Retrospecting on their love, Michael thinks. "[...] but it was when she played by herself, to herself—a suite, say, or an invention, or a fugue—that I had almost completely yielded my being to her" (83). With Julia it is likewise, though she reveals it inadvertently, when Michael asks her why she does not wear a wedding ring. She says, "I don't know. It distracts me when I play the piano. I look at it and I can't concentrate on the music" (109).

Though she is married to another man, Michael relishes the consolation that "I know her uniquely as this man who lives with her cannot—in the core of her being; the great fraying cord that links her to her music" (168).

Music aside, their love, though evident enough on the purely physical level, vibrates with a touch of transcendence that elevates them above anything sordid and contrives to keep them innocent somehow. In one of the novel's most poignant exchanges, Seth fields the moral question with great delicacy:

> [...] She smiles, a little sadly. 'Making music and making love—it's a bit too easy an equation.'
>
> 'Have you told him (the husband) about me?' I ask.
>
> 'No,' she says. 'I don't know what to do about all this subterfuge: faxes in German, coming up to see you here.'
>
> [...] but it's really Luke (the son) who I feel I'm [...]
>
> 'Betraying?'
>
> 'I'm afraid of all these words. They're so blunt and fierce [...]' (136).

When Michael first sees Julia on the bus and subsequently fails to find her, his world ceases to turn. Seth depicts the depth of Michael's emotion brilliantly, not through a direct description but even more effectively by looking for an echo of those feelings in Julia: "Was she standing on the pavement somewhere, scanning the multitude and crying?" (44).

Julia, in spite of her conflicting loyalties, is as powerless as is Michael to resist sinking into the tangled beauty of their love. The ghost of Vienna is persistent and she too is haunted by the past, although she does make an attempt to get on with her life. But as far as social norms are concerned, Michael knows that:

> Adultery and sin: ludicrously, there are no gentle words [...] what if we were not making love together, we whose blood beats in one pulse? How touching it would be, how chaste, sad, poignant, beautiful—how self congratulatory, how false, how agonizing, how comfortless (169-70).

The simplicity with which Seth considers and dismisses these words—adultery and sin—goes a long way in ascertaining the complexity of the relationship between Michael and Julia, where emotions run too deep to be reduced to the tawdriness that these words imply. Michael observes, with some surprise, "What is wrong with my conscience, that I can feel worried for her but not guilty?" (188).

However, confronted with the radiance of Julia's family life, Michael realizes that he cannot tear her away: "Photographs, paintings, books, carpets, curtains, cushions—a populated room, a life as solid as rock" (210).

So in Vienna, he eagerly grasps what Julia is willing to give of herself: "shared time is better than none. Why taint such sporadic joy with long views before and after?" (233).

In Venice they come full circle, and it is as if the past ten tears have never been. Yet, the outside world constantly impinges into their shared circle of bliss, in the forms of James and Luke. When Julia refers to Luke as "my poor baby," the hopelessness of their relationship suddenly dawns on Michael: "I feel a sudden surge of resentment against this poor baby. How can I ever compete with him? How could I even think of drawing them apart?" (276).

Trapped between divided loyalties, Julia breaks out in an anguished "if only there were two of me" (287). The bell finally tolls for their doomed romance when Julia once again faces life head on and tells Michael, "I, of all people, who have a Before and an After, should have known that you cannot relive your life" (325). She realizes that she can never stop loving Michael but accepts that each must tread a different path.

Music and love are thus the two major themes in the novel, which is appropriate, considering that both love and music play on the emotions. It is interesting how Seth weaves the two together to create a canvas on which the passions are so consummately depicted—obsessive love, lives spent trying to recapture perfection—to the degree that reading the novel does not amount to a mere reading, it becomes an empathic experience by virtue of Seth's brilliant apprehension of it. Like life itself, the novel resounds with the complex and often painful episode of life's events.

But Michael's and Julia's is not the only relationship in the novel. The love stories between humans and music, instruments, dead composers, even the cities in which their music is played, are equally gripping and convincing. This is why music usurps love's place as central theme. The characters not only love each other for the music they make, but also their passion for and their devotion to their music outlasts their travails and escapades by far.

Michael's relationship with his violin has been realized with a rare insight. Michael loves it, and the bond between them is strong. He tells Mrs. Formby (who has lent the violin to him), "I didn't tell you, did I, that we're going to Venice after Vienna? So I'll be taking it back to its birth place for a visit. That should make it happy?" (69). When he takes the violin home to Vivaldi's church, where it was played two centuries ago in another life, and they find the doors barred, Michael says, "I can feel my Tononi moping. It is too much" (267). When they do get to play inside, they choose the Largo of Vivaldi's first Manchester sonata and Michael feels that "nothing lovelier has ever been written for the instrument, and my violin clearly feels it has been written personally for it—for it to play here" (269).

The shadow of the thought that Mrs. Formby's heirs will demand the violin back after she is dead hangs heavy over Michael's head. Michael reflects, "We have been together for twelve years. Its sound is my sound. I can't bear to part with it" (69). After Mrs. Formby's death he tries desperately to engrave every remaining second spent with the violin into his sensations: "Tune the strings though. Play scales. More than father, mother, friend or lover, it has companioned you [...]. Remove the chinrest, feel its wood again" (354).

When the dreaded letter from Rochdale finally arrives, Michael takes out the violin with a heavy heart, to play it one last time, and one can feel the sadness that is overwhelming him almost palpably. Not only Michael, but also all the other musicians empathize greatly with their respective instruments.

Schubert is ugly, but kissable nonetheless for the music he has made. There is great joy in playing Beethoven's Opus 104 (quintet for strings): "How good it is to play this quintet, to play it, not to work at it—to play for our own joy, with no need to convey anything to anyone outside our ring of recreation" (79). This kind of empathy with the world of music is the *raison d' etre* of *An Equal Music.*

The character development in this novel is exceptionally well done. At first glance, Michael, with his idiosyncrasies, his selfishness, hypersensitivity, his weak inner self, is not particularly likeable. His mental processes are directed inward, shutting out the view of the world outside, festering in a mire of bitterness, self-resentment, and to a certain extent, self-pity. Even his affair with his student Virginie portrays him in a negative light, underscoring his inability to see much beyond himself and his own preoccupied feelings. But all these faults are redeemed by his innate goodness, honesty, and above all, by his passion for music and for Julia, a passion that is quite beyond the grasp of lesser mortals. It is a yardstick of Seth's talent that the reader empathizes with Michael's pain even as Seth reveals Michael's narcissism.

Michael lives his life in a sort of waking dream which is a strange medley of past associations and current events. A clear, cold, blue skied day makes him say, "I can smell the professor on a day like this" (15). This after ten tears. It is largely due to this haunted nature of his life that Michael joins the water-serpents, acknowledging with his characteristic candidness that the atmosphere in the club house "admitted me to a world outside Archangel Court and the Maggiore quartet and Virginie's flat and the ungiving pressure of my thoughts" (22).

Seth reveals Michael's character through his interactions with the people in his life. The reason he left Vienna becomes clear when his teacher, Carl Käll, points out that Michael is very self willed. Michael accepts this: "Carl Käll [...] did not, unaided, drive me from Vienna. It was as much my younger self, unyielding, unwilling to change a mentor for a dictator, or to sidle past a collision" (18). Theirs is a complex relationship that Michael, only in retrospect, can see in its true perspective: "When he played I heard a sound so noble—round, warm, unaffected—that I wanted to emulate it, but when I tried his techniques they did violence to my own style. Why could he not permit me to form myself—with guidance, not constraint?" (108).

Michael's devotion to his art is distilled out of the nobility of his soul. On discovering Beethoven's opus 104, he tell the reader, in anticipation of musical ecstasy, "Late tonight, after the rehearsal, I'll come home, light a candle, lie down on my duvet, and sink into the quintet" (40). Remembering the first time he ever heard chamber music—Barbirolli conducting an orchestra—he says, "He brings down a stick and a huge and lovely noise fills the world. More than anything else I want to be part of such a noise" (67).

The affair with Julia perhaps reveals him better than anything else. After losing her, his movements become automated; the effort involved in taking control of his life is simply beyond him: "The one fixed point in my week is my saturday morning swim. If I lapse here, I will lose all pattern to my days" (51). And yet he underestimates himself when he tells Julia that he will not be able to cope without her, for in the course of the novel he grows out of his erstwhile selfishness into a more forgiving and altruistic mindset. He comes to realize that he must not tear Julia away from her son, and accepts that their love will find its consummation only in the music that they will play.

In creating Michael, Seth has created a man with a flaw. This flaw is a mental one, and it manifests itself in Michael's fingers during moments of intense emotional excitement, and in his social isolation. Seth agrees and adds:

> Yes, and in a kind of attitude towards authority or what he sees as authoritarianism and perhaps a lack of comprehension of himself and those people of whom he is particularly fond of or who he loves, wiiom he's obsessing about.[10]

About Michael's creation Seth says, "It was odd to create Michael. He is not a nasty character. In many ways he's honorable. He's liked by plenty of nice people and they don't seem to give up on him."[11] For Seth, character is at the very heart of the novel. He does not try to be the author, to be Vikram Seth, if the character he has created wants to be different, and particularly in the case of Michael, when the character has a voice in the first person. Seth explains this particular difficulty:

> [...] once you've decided to write in the first person, you're stuck with that character's voice, and that character's blindness, and that character's percipience, and that character's views about all sorts of things. And if Michael is a difficult person, you've got to go along with that.[12]

The reason for writing a narrative in the first person was two fold: first, the subject matter itself—music, about which Seth says that "the only way to get into the music through words is to describe the thoughts of someone who is actually a musician himself."[13] The second reason was "the immediacy of the intensity of someone's feelings when he is in an imperfect firmament. That interested me very much, especially in an intense love story."[14]

Michael sees the darker side of his own personality with surprising clarity. "[...] A volatility, a sense of resistance, of scepticism, roughness, impulsiveness, even, at times, of dark panic, almost brainsickness" (81). This is entirely true, but then the major characters in a novel do not have to be perfect, or even lovable. As long as they are recognizable as real, and are capable of drawing some sort of emotion from the reader, they justify their creation. Michael is just such a character.

For Michael, music becomes a substitute, both for love and religion. The remark that he makes at the end of the novel about the controlling power of music is something that Seth says Michael needs as a philosophy because music takes him out of himself in an inexplicable way, out of the selfishness that a spirit like him is prone to.

With Julia, music is as much of a religion as it is with Michael, but other things matter to her as well: her family, her child. When Michael leaves Vienna, she is truly heartbroken, but pulls herself together to pick up the pieces of her life. Seth leads us to believe that were it not for her deafness, she would indeed have coped quite well. But with her impending loss of hearing (loss of music) and owing to the fact that her affair with Michael is unfinished business, she is drawn to him in an almost hypnotic trance. At one point, she utters a wrenching, "Why did you leave me?" (279). Later she reproaches herself for being "so selfish, so self indulgent, so reckless" (328), and gives up Michael though it is even harder the second time around.

Julia's deafness is an angle that evinces Seth's courage in exploring the idea of a deaf musician—about being under the threat of losing music from a life that is dedicated to music. The character of Julia is based on famous deaf percussionist Evelyn Glennie, who Seth once dined with and was amazed to discover later she was deaf. He was then in the early stages of writing *An Equal Music*, and the idea of a deaf musician had its appeal. Seth explains that after he had decided to bring Julia's deafness into the novel, he found a number of musicians who were quiet hard of hearing. Also, he interviewed doctors about deafness, so that the pacing of the onset of the disease was correct. He also took lip reading classes for thirteen weeks, in order to have a better understanding of how people who cannot cope with their ears cope through their eyes and in the case of musicians, also through the mind's ear.[15]

Unfolding Julia's deafness in a series of clues, Seth describes her as she tries to cope. Very well portrayed is the insensitivity of people towards deaf persons, in spite of their best intentions. Seth also reveals in a quiet manner the response of people upon learning of Julia's disability. Strangely enough, her fellow musicians are more accommodating of her deafness, probably because they realize that when it comes to music there is a realm of mystery and a half-heard and half-imagined sound anyway. How could Beethoven have composed all those sonatas otherwise?

Seth does not seek to make Julia's deafness a metaphor for any other aspect of the novel. It is to be taken at face value; it is there, just as it is often there in real life. It is certainly more tragic since she is a musician, but resiliently, she allows her musical instincts to guide her back into proper musical functioning. Both Michael and Julia are very intense characters, and it is in large measure due to Seth's verbal dexterity that the novel accurately conveys a great deal of the emotion it inspires.

Among other noteworthy things in the novel is the depiction of Michael's provincial boyhood at Rochdale in the north of England. The portrayal of a disadvantaged childhood in a decaying and industrialized landscape, the uprooting of human settlements, the ill and aging father fixated on the family cat with the characteristic pathos-inducing loneliness of the very old, the gradual ebbing away of the life-blood of the town—all of it is skilfully delineated:

> The handsome town hall presides over a waste—it is a town with its heart torn out. Everything speaks of its decline. Over the course of a century [...] it lost its work and its wealth. Then came the planning blight: the replacement of human slums by inhuman ones, the marooning of churches in traffic islands, the building of precincts where once there were shops. Finally, two decades of garrotting from the government in London, and everything civic or social was choked of funds: schools, libraries, hospitals, transport. The town which had been the home of the co-operative movement lost its sense of community (71).

Also remarkable is Seth's marvellous sense of place, which entails in this instance the ability to conjure up visual spaces through aural cues. Seth has the knack for bringing a place to life by homing in on its uniqueness, and in this novel, this uniqueness is in what the place sounds like. The rising song of a lark evokes the moors of Rochdale; London is represented by the songs of robins in winter and blackbirds in summer and by pigeons, Vienna is conjured up by the sound of nightingales, and Venice by the music of Vivaldi. Seth thus authenticates the novel by linking the profession of the characters with their sonic perception of the world.

As always with Seth, much of the pleasure that the novel provides is in its detail and unhurried pace. The description of London parks, long walks, the account of the water-serpents, London flat life, and the portrayal of the concierge: all add to the novel's texture rather than to its meaning. There are long descriptions of Venice and Vienna, and few readers will grudge Seth that, owing to the excellence of his style, which in this novel is deeply evocative and emotional, yet sparse, highly appropriate when the characters are so intense. It comes as near to conveying the mercurial moods of love and of music as is possible in words.

When music or profound emotions surface, the prose becomes almost musical. Assonance, alliteration, rhythm and cadence, syncopated sentences with short words, lento with long, vowel-filled words—all are used to achieve this effect. When Seth talks of Bach's great, unfinished, mysterious *Art of the Fugue* or when he thinks of Venice or Schubert, it is as if the novel existed in another, higher dimension. The plot is by no means particularly enthralling but in modern writing it is the style, not the substance that counts. The book acquires literary stature on account of Seth's masterly handling. He gets the music right and the love right too. It is perhaps justifiable then that John Carey, the eminent English critic, has summed up his eulogy of *An Equal Music* with these words of Tennyson, "Deep as first love, and wild with all regret."[16]

There is also a "determined inter-textuality to Seth's writing in this book."[17] Employed at moments of high emotional intensity, these literary or biblical references seek to create an objective correlative for Michael's state of mind, which at these times is high-strung and desperate. Having failed to catch up with Julia, Michael tells us in Piccadilly Circus, "Under the arrow of Eros I suit down and weep" (43). London monuments and Michael's desperation are thus fused in an echo of psalm 137 and its many subsequent literary adaptations.[18] At Rochdale, conversation about births, deaths, divorces and escapades draws from Michael's sensitive soul the words, again in a biblical echo, "for better for worse, unto us a child, ashes to ashes" (63). Later he talks of "the swift ellipses of the earth" (223), wonders of a dog in a Carpaccio painting that "did he who make the dragon make thee?" (278). As the novel draws towards its finale and Michael sinks deeper and deeper into despair and his suffering intensifies, these references become increasingly frequent and are accompanied by a fragmentation in thought that is reproduced in a stream-of-consciousness manner, moving from past to present and vice versa without warning, often mixing up both, conjuring up brilliantly the half-sane and half-fractured state of Michael's mind.

Due to the aforementioned quality, *An Equal Music* is as much a novel about love and music as about a certain inner darkness. It has a melancholic strain that manifests itself in the isolation of the characters, in Michael's obsessions, Julia's deafness, in a lack of common perspectives; even the humour is dark, serving chiefly to make the tragic parts more poignant by contrast, along with the goal of providing 'dramatic relief', to borrow a term from Shakespearean criticism, as the story grows almost suffocatingly sad. Seth is sagaciously wary of sustaining the novel at that intense pitch for all of its 381 pages, yet this novel is not for the faint-hearted, or for those who are afraid to acknowledge their passions.

The conclusion of the novel is even-handed and utterly believable, with Michael holding on, not to Julia, but to a shared memory. When he hears Julia playing, to him "it is a beauty beyond imagining—clear, lovely. Inexorable, phrase across phrase, phrase echoing phrase, the incomplete, the unending Art of Fugue. It is an equal music" (380). The philosophy of aestheticism inherent in these closing lines marks a moment of epiphany for him, making him realize that "Music, such music is a sufficient gift. Why ask for happiness; why hope not to grieve? It is enough, it is to be blessed enough, to live from day to day and hear such music—not too much, or the soul could not sustain it—from time to time" (381). At the heart of this epiphany stands Bach's great fugue. In Spanish the word *fuga* means a "musical composition in counterpoint, based on the use of imitation of a short, but well differentiated theme,"[19] and the *punto de fuga* is the point in a drawing done in perspective where straight parallel lines converge. The ending of the novel thus becomes the punto de fuga, "the point at which in art, straight parallel lines converge, due to perspective."[20] This is because at the end of the novel, Michael is alone like he was in the beginning, but there is one important difference: his thoughts have reached a resolution and he is no longer troubled. He has learned acceptance and it has brought him serenity. This change in perspective has enabled him to come to terms with his past, made the present bearable, and the future promising. And perhaps most essentially of all, he has realized that to be complete is an advantage, not a necessity.

The title of the novel is taken from an apt sermon by Donne, Epigraphed to the novel, the sermon reads:

> And into that gate they shall enter, and in that house they shall dwell, where there shall be no cloud or sun, no darkness nor dazzling, but one equal light, no noise nor silence, but one equal music, no fears nor hopes, but one equal possession, no foes nor friends, but one equal communion and identity, no ends or beginnings, but one equal eternity (Epigraph).

Here "equal" becomes a synonym for the divine, for something that is perfect beyond imagining. The title fits in very well with the spirit of the novel: the music of the masters is an equal music to Michael's ears, for it enables him to temporarily touch this divinity and gives his soul sustenance to go on. And not only is the music an equal one, but the love, as envisioned by Seth, grows into an equal, perfect love, marked by balance and equability, understanding and acceptance.

The novel thus reiterates Seth's earlier philosophy of the value of such mundane institutions as home and family. It is a story about the ultimate triumph of sanity over human irrationality, and a seeking to create a balance between personal and artistic worlds. It explores loneliness, especially the loneliness of an artist, and seeks to portray the interface of creativity with the unavoidable tensions of daily life. It is also about the joy of having regained what was thought to be lost forever, coupled with the anguish of realization and denial. It is impassioned and poetic, elegiac and witty by turns, and set against the Augustan backdrop of Venice and Vienna, it is a fit stage for the unfurling of a love tale to the music of Beethoven and Bach. Seth's obvious passion for his subject and his subsequent empathy with it lend this novel an extra dimension. This, together with his talent for words and imagery and an excellent literary ending make this novel an exceptional read.

Vikram Seth received the Crosswords Book award for *An Equal Music* in 1999.

Notes

1. Vikram Seth, "Writers on Writing," Radio series transcript, *Australian Broadcasting Corporation*, URL:http://www.abc.net.au/writers/writesummary.htm
2. *An Equal Music*, Viking Penguin India, 1999, 166.
3. Bernhard Holland, *New York Times*, n.d.
4. Salman Rushdie, *The Ground Beneath Her Feet*, New York: Henry Holt and Company, 1999.
5. J.W.N. Sullivan, Beethoven, *His Spiritual Development*, Vintage Books (A Division of Random House), New York, 1960, 4, 6.
6. Peter Lowe, *The Voice of The Turtle*, www.voiceoftheturtle.org/reviews/book/peter-seth.html
7. Sarah Bryan, "Author Seth Rhapsodizes on a String Quartet," *St. Louis Post Dispatch*, Jun. 10, 1999.
8. Lynn Carey, "Seth Draws on his Emotional Past to Create Characters," *Times Book,* Club Interview, July 30, 2000.
9. David Blake, "Me and My Fiddle," *Al-Ahram Weekly*, 9-15 Sept., 1999, issue no. 446.
10. Jay Curie and Michèle Denis, "Hearing a Different Tune," *January Magazine* Interview, June 1999.
11. *Ibid.*
12. "Writers on Writing," *loc cit.*
13. Kohli, *loc cit.*
14. Sara Crowe, "No Ice, Vikram," *A Talk at the Seymour Centre, the University of Sydney News*, March 23, 2000
15. Ruth Alexander and Isabella Perriera, "Dark Lord of the Seth," Cherwell—*The Independent Oxford University Newspaper*. URL:www.planet-hardcore-/cherwell/archive/ht00/3/features/6.html
16. John Carey, "Review of An Equal Music," *The Sunday Times*, London, March 28, 1999.
17. Tim Parks, "A Sentimental Education," *New York Book Review*, July 15, 1999.
18. Parks, *loc cit.*
19. *El Pequeno Larousse Ilustrado*, 469, 1996 ed.
20. Fausta, URL:www.barnesandnoble.com/bookshelf/fiction/best1.asp

6

Literary Digressions

As the title suggests, in this chapter will be analyzed works that stand in a category of their own, each being one of a kind in the matter of genre. Each work discussed here reaffirms the fact that Seth writes primarily for his own pleasure, when and where the muse takes him, and that he is not heir to the superiority inherited by those writers who will write only in a particular genre, deeming other ones to be unfit for their notice.

I. *FROM HEAVEN LAKE*

Although travelogue-writing has existed in all languages right from the burgeoning of literature, it has become popular only in recent years. Prior to the latter half of the twentieth century, travelogues were few and far between. Consequently, as a genre, travelogue writing invited hardly any literary criticism until eminent writers like Eric Newby, Pico Iyer, Graham Greene, V.S. Naipaul, Frank Delaney, Dan Jacobson, Dervla Murphy, Vikram Seth, J.M. Coetzee, and Michael Ondaatje, among others enriched it with their contributions. Travel writing, which was previously viewed as being unworthy of analytical study by dint of it's not meeting the standards of literature, has thus slowly been emerging as a genre worth its salt, "especially for scholars looking at the representation of culture(s) in literature."[1] The increasing number of new publications in this genre along with academic interest in it evinces this trend.

Vikram Seth's award-winning travelogue is based on a journal maintained by him during the course of a 1981 hitchhiking trip home to India from China, via Tibet & Nepal. Seth was a student in China's Nanjing University during the years 1980–82, on an Economics research scholarship supported by the Ford Foundation at Stanford University. In the summer of 1981, Seth and other fellow students had been taken on a sight seeing trip to the Sinkiang province of China, in China's north-western desert. A chance singing of the song "Maine Awara Hoon," the theme song from the Indian block buster movie "Awara," in front of Chinese officials won Seth a travel permit for Lhasa by road, which was a rarity since foreigners were generally severely restricted in their movements in China and individual forays into travelling were discouraged. Seth however had always wanted to visit Tibet, and having got Lhasa stamped on his travel pass by the aforementioned good luck, he found himself hitching a ride in a truck across four Chinese provinces to travel home, against the dictates of both his finances and good sense. This journey was later shaped into the travelogue called *From Heaven Lake.*

In *From Heaven Lake*, Seth harnesses his remarkable power of observation and blends it with the artistic sensibility to take the reader on an unforgettable journey through the most mysterious and least explored region of Asia. The flavour of the book in enhanced by the spice of a subdued sense of excitement and danger, resulting from hitchhiking through forbidden areas, neatly side-stepping "guiding" (Chinese regulations, to break which is sacrilege in China), and above all by the landscape itself—varied, desolate and bleak, unfriendly, yet breathtaking in its beauty—crossing four Chinese provinces: the north western desert of Xinjiang and Gansu, the basin and plateau of Qinghai, and finally, the mountains of Tibet. In the course of his journey, Seth introduces the reader to the various nationalities inside China: Han-Chinese who form a majority of the population; Uighurs, who are Muslims and ethnically closer to the Turks than to the Hans; and Tibetans, who have an ancient culture of their own.

From Heaven Lake is an ideal piece of travel writing, delineating the geographical, socio-economic, and cultural features of the region in their totality, without being clouded with issues of identity (usually a big issue with post-colonial writers). This latter fact makes the narrative light in tone, in happy contrast with works that tend to grapple with post-colonialism ad nauseam. The reason for this is that Seth is at home anywhere in the world; the aspect of the world being a global village is more real to him than is the aspect of a post-colonial existence.

In the travelogue, Seth does not take pains to set himself apart as a 'traveller,' as opposed to being a mere 'tourist.' The distinction is a fine one and most travelogue writers subscribe to it to a greater or lesser degree, viewing 'tourism' in an offhandedly derogatory manner. Seth's goal, however, was not to follow in the literary footsteps of travel writers—he only wanted to experience and perceive, get the feel of the country, and to see it first hand instead of jetting above it on a homeward-bound flight. Writing a book about his travels was never at any point his initial goal. As a result, both his manner and style are refreshing. However, from the book one can discern that it is written in the spirit of a true traveller. A tourist accustomed to Thomas Cook tours would never hitchhike and even if he did he would probably constantly complain about the inconveniences and the hardships of travelling cross-country in an unplanned and spur-of-the-moment manner. Seth, on the other hand, finds the beauty despite the hardships, is consistently uncomplaining of what must have been extremely trying circumstances, and even when accosted by strangers and hampered by unforeseen delays, manages to take it all in his stride, intent on his goal to see Lhasa unhindered by closely monitored tourist excursions.

There are two additional advantages that Seth wields over the average travelogue writer: the first one is that before embarking on this journey Seth had already learned how to comprehend Chinese, both written and spoken. This facilitated communication and rounded off the sharp edges of 'foreignness' to a great extent, in addition to dispensing with the necessity of travelling in groups or with guides. Thus, Seth made friends of natives everywhere: in the market place, in a mosque, travelling along the road and so on. It was only in Tibet that he found himself unable to communicate with people who spoke only Tibetan and no Chinese. Secondly, the avoiding of organized modes of travel and hitch hiking in their stead lead to a wider variety of experience and close encounters with the local people during the journey that would have been virtually impossible otherwise. Seth's training as an economist imparts an additional dimension to the book, for he tends to see things not only in their immediate perspective but also in their wider economic and political significance. It is due to this reason that he often digresses towards the economic and political infrastructure of China, inevitably comparing it with that of India.

D. Maya says, "As a record of subjective expressions, the tone of the discourse in travel-writing is determined by the persona of the travel-writer: the land is transformed according to the perceiving, narrating self."[2] Subscribing to this premise, *From Heaven Lake* assumes great importance, for it becomes a reliable index to Seth's personality. This is therefore the book that reveals more about Seth that even his poetry does and although not written in the nature of an auto-biography, this book nevertheless bares before the reader many facets of Seth's personality.

The most striking feature that emerges from this book is that Seth burns incense at the shrine of beauty, taking an almost Keats-like pleasure in it. Whether it is the beauty of form made by the human hand, the beauty of colour in Nature, or even the beauty of sound as experienced in the cadence of flute music, beauty never fails to leave him profoundly moved. To quote instances in point at several places in the book: about Heaven Lake, the Lake that lends its name to the travelogue, Seth proclaims that it is "and area of such natural beauty that I could live here, content, for a year."[3] By self–admittance, Seth finds himself in kinship with the Chinese sage Confucius, who's idea of bliss is to bathe in the river Yi during late spring and then to go home, chanting poetry. As is Seth's style, most of the Nature-descriptions in the book have been written with the intent to convey the image that has captivated Seth as graphically as possible. For instance while describing sunset in the deserts of Dunhuang, he says:

> Above, the sky, marked with a few residual clouds, changes to a deep red, and the sun sinks over the vague horizon of the desert. For a few minutes afterwards, the underside of the clouds reflects a sun already invisible, and by a strange tilt of light the sky actually appears to become brighter. Then the angle changes, the clouds turn grey, and above me is a sky of deep indigo. In this desert night the Milky way is brilliantly clear. It strikes me how descriptive of its meandering course is its Chinese name, the Silver River (62).

Occasionally he lapses into a spontaneous outburst, delineating experience as event, as in: "The sunset tonight in this vapid flat-roofed town is beautiful-tufts of pink and bands of yellow at the close, and the freshness of skies washed by rain" (49), or when he says, about a lake in Nanhu, "the lake in cool, but warm bands sketch sensuously across it" (69). About the Chaidam basin he says, "The landscape is so spectacular that I seem hardly to have noticed our more mundane activities today" (75). Of his first glimpse of the Potala Palace in Lhasa: "In this late afternoon light it is so beautiful that I cannot speak at all" (117). Of Nilamu:

> A land of streams! Some, like a downward smoke,
> Slow—dropping veils of thinnest lawn, did go—
>
> And across the valley against the grey verticality of a cliff a thin strand of water indeed vanishes into a mist or smoke atomised by the wind, to reappear, reconstituted from, it seems, the air itself into a liquid skein of light. There is enchantment in flowing water: I sit hypnotized by its beauty—water, the most unifying of the elements, that ties land and sea and air in one living ring (165).

On hearing flute–music in the market-place in Kathmandu, Seth says:

> I find it difficult to tear myself away from the square. Flute music always does this to me: it is at once the most universal and most particular of sounds [...] to hear any flute is, it seems to me, to be drawn into the commonality of all mankind, to be moved by music closest in its phrases and sentences to the human voice (176).

Throughout the book Seth displays this sense of reverent wonder at the beauty around him, whether it is the beauty scattered by God's own hand or by the hand of man.

This book also reveals what can be termed as Seth's wide human sympathy. Seth says, "When I think of China, I think first of my friends and only then of Qin Shi Huang's tomb" (36). This is significant, because beauty in all forms touches a chord deep within Seth, and to admit that friendship has precedence over it is to say a lot. All the people that he comes in contact with are not disembodied people without names and faces—he stops to say hello and to individualize them, even while describing types. It is not surprising then, that he makes friends every where he goes. People and their idiosyncrasies interest him, and to his credit, he never displays a sense of superiority over anyone, in any way. For example, about an impoverished household in Nanhu he writes:

> At the house, the mother is breast-feeding the insatiable baby. Her six-year-old niece looks on and laughs. From defiant curiosity and dread of me she has progressed to friendly mimicry. She is called Xiexie, and has small plaits. Together we watch three boys unload cartloads of sand by the wall outside the house. They then drive the donkey—carts on with cries of 'kirrick! kirrick!' A wall is to be built nearby, or perhaps this wall is to be strengthened: Xiexie only speaks the local dialect and I can catch perhaps one word in three of her explanation (71).

The various observations about Sui, the Chinese truck-driver who gave Seth a lift, and two other travelling companions: Xio San and Gyanseng, all reveal a genuine sense of bonding with other humans. The following remark made about Sui is curiously true of Seth himself, "He has a way of treating people as individuals rather than as representatives of types that precludes any sense of cultural superiority" (74).

This instinctive humanity extends itself to Seth's thinking. He sees himself first as a human being, devoid of all other racial associations. That is to say, he bonds with other people on a primal, human level, regardless of ethnicity, creed, or nationality. At several places in the book he has expressed the sentiment that nationality has nothing to do with the solidarity of human bonding: as when he is describing a night spent by Gyanseng, Sui, and himself, in Sui's truck:

> Here we three, cooped, alone,
> Tibetan, Indian, Han,
> Against a common dawn
> Catch what poor sleep we can,
> And sleeping drag the same
> Sparse air into our lungs,
> And dreaming each of home
> Sleep talk in different tongues (98).

A natural corollary of this sympathetic and broadminded attitude is the distress Seth feels as he records the changes wrought by the Chinese Cultural Revolution that brutalised the ancient cultural heritage of China under the leadership of Chairman Mao and fostered a generation of fanatics brought up on Mao's dictums. The flight of the Dalai Lama from Tibet, the suppression of native Tibetans, the Tiananmen Square massacre (the latter in the foreword to the 1990 edition of the book), all are recorded with a keenly felt sympathy. The drawbacks and tyrannies of Imperialism are analysed and especially the plight of indigenous Tibetans after Chinese occupation of Tibet is registered with a pang of sympathy. Taking this feeling to an international level Seth muses:

> If India and China were amicable towards each other, almost half the world would be at peace. Yet friendship rests on understanding; and the two countries, despite their contiguity, have had almost no contact in the course of history [...] neither strong economic interest nor the natural affinities of a common culture tie India and China together.

> [...]. The best that can be hoped for on a national level is a respectful patience on either side [...] (178).

The feeling of global brotherhood is reinforced in the following lines, when Seth in meditating on the nature of the water element: "The solid substances of the earth more easily cohere to particular people or nations, but those that flow—air, water—are communal even within our lives" (166), or as in:

> [...] to learn about another great culture is to enrich one's life, to understand one's own country better, to feel more at home in the world, and indirectly to add to that reservoir of individual goodwill that may, generations from now, temper the cynical use of national power (178).

All these ruminations set the tone of the travelogue, making it so much than just a travel book. Seth's musings on Chinese and Indian politics and Economics, on poverty and authoritarianism—all topics inescapable for a South Asian economist, are interesting, to say the least. They are the products of an insightful mind that has the ability to penetrate to the core of things to perceive them in their totality.

Stylistically, this travelogue brings out clearly the fact that Seth's prose is adequate, not only for a travel book but also for the purpose of novelistic description. All through the book, Seth incessantly describes: the landscape, the people, their culture and customs and language; and these descriptions are interspersed with purely subjective perceptions and experiences. Not only the people mentioned, but even the places described assume a personality of their own, as Seth vividly conjures up an atmosphere around them.

The book opens with a description of a sultry July morning in Turfan, and within the first paragraph, Seth manages to communicate to the reader the very essence of the place:

> The flies have entered the bus, and their buzzing adds to the overwhelming sense of heat. We drive through the town first: a few two-storey buildings of depressing concrete, housing government offices or large shops-foodstores,

> clothing, hardware. Small street stalls too, with their wares displayed on the pavement and vendors selling refreshments-glasses of bilious yellow and red liquids, looking increasingly attractive as our thirst builds. Donkey—carts pulled by tired looking donkeys, pestered by flies and enervated by the dry, breezeless heat, some ridden by boys with white skullcaps, others standing beside a pile of water melons. Even when they flick their tails they do so listlessly. It is not long past dawn, and already the heat has struck. And the light, shining on walls and signs—in Chinese, Latin and Arabic scripts has a painful brilliance (1).

Among the many descriptions in the book are those about Xinjiang province, which is the land of mountain fed crystal streams that network under ground (called "karez"), Tian Chi (Heaven Lake), which is a beautiful haven for those seeking solitude set in the very lap of Nature; Xian, that is reminiscent of Delhi in its layout, weather and rich historical heritage.

The style of narration is characteristic of Seth's technique, where he observes every thing around him first with a purely objective eye and proceeds to subjectify it by correlating it with his past. An interesting self-analytical passage from the book brings this out clearly:

> Increasingly of late, and particularly when I drink, I find my thoughts drawn into the past rather than impelled into the future. I recall drinking sherry in California and dreaming of my earlier student days in England, where I ate dalmoth and dreamed of Delhi. What is the purpose, I wonder, of all this restlessness? I sometimes seem to my self to wander around the world merely accumulating material for future nostalgias (35).

In this book, there is perfect balance between the elements that comprise pure travel writing and the ones that do not. All other thoughts are skilfully woven around the basic theme of travelling home. Seth keeps remembering his family, is glad that they have not stopped writing to him, and despite having lived abroad for several years, still thinks of India as home. As the journey enters its final stages, there is a longing to be home, which is implicit in the some what hasty conclusion:

> I consider what route I should take back home. If I were propelled by enthusiasm for travel *per se*, I would go by bus and train to Patna, then sail up the Ganges past Banares to Allahabad. Then up the Jumna, past Agra to Delhi. But I am exhausted and homesick; today is the last day of August. Go home, I tell myself: move directly towards home. I enter a Nepal Airlines office and buy a ticket for tomorrow's flight (176).

Throughout the book the reader is made aware of the passage of time and how it hangs heavy over Seth's head. His Lhasa travel permit will expire soon and he must leave China before then. This, coupled with the delay created by unforeseen bureaucratic red tape and natural calamities keeps both reader and writer on tenterhooks until Seth reaches Nepal.

In this manner, the book partakes of all the elements of travel: homesickness, the difficulty of travelling over an inhospitable terrain, the differences encountered in food, clothing, and lifestyle, and other factors which are simply beyond one's control. All the aforementioned characteristics smoothly coalesce to make *From Heaven Lake* an extremely well-written travelogue. Seth's narrative style is immensely readable and well in keeping with the casual theme of sightseeing, although Seth's sensitivity to his surroundings detracts considerably from the casualness. This is brought out especially in two episodes: the Tibetan funereal rite of chopping the dead body, mixing it with meal, and feeding it to eagles, as seen at the Sera monastery in Tibet, and the visit to the Potala Palace, the erstwhile winter palace of the Dalai Lama. Of the latter Seth says, "So fervid and overwhelming is the experience that when I am finally extruded into the sunlit exit, I find myself trembling" (137).

The book thus alternates between objective perception and subjective delineation of the sights encountered during the journey. This saves the book from being merely a well-written travel documentary and moulds it into a delicate blend of fact and the author's own perceptive reality that makes for very interesting reading and actually reveals far more about this region than any run-of-the-mill travel book would. Among the salient features of this travelogue are the descriptions of the sights and sounds encountered during the journey, affecting almost photographic realism, the persona of the writer himself—keen on apprehending an alien culture, and the fact that his voice in the travelogue always rings true.

II. *ARION AND THE DOLPHIN*

Vikram Seth was commissioned by the Baylis Programme at the English National Opera to write the accompanying opera text for 'Arion and the Dolphin,' the music for which was provided by Alec Roth. The libretto was published in 1994, to coincide with the first performance of the opera in June 1994. The opera is in nine scenes, for professionals and community performers.

The tale of 'Arion and the Dolphin' is closely based on the following classical tales: In Shakespeare's *Twelfth Night*,[4] mention is made of Arion, a rich poet and musician who had his life threatened by pirates on board his ship. His last will was to sing one final song, and since he must die, he wished to jump overboard, taking his own life. After a very high-pitched, long, wailing song, Arion jumped overboard. But he did not drown. A dolphin carried him about 200 miles to shore. The Greeks say that this is true and happened when Pereander was king (about 60 B.C.). This incident was also reported by the historian Herodotus and others.[5]

The story in Seth's version in approximately the same. Arion leaves his home town of Corinth, then ruled by Pereander, to participate in a singing competition in Sicily, on pain on death if he does not win. He wins the competition, but while he is sailing back to Corinth, the boatmen on his ship decide to murder him to get at the riches he has won. Arion pleads to be allowed to sing one last song and then jumps into the sea; he is then rescued by a school of dolphins and brought back to Corinth. One of the dolphins becomes very attached to him during the journey to Corinth and decides to stay with him. However, Arion is imprisoned because his prize having been looted, he cannot prove that he had won and the dolphin is forced to perform tricks for a show, where it pines for Arion.

By the time Pereander realizes his mistake and frees Arion, the dolphin is dead.

The story is recounted with Seth's inimitable charm, and his superb facility with rhyme. The story is essentially tragic but Seth keeps the dark clouds at bay until the very end. The only grim episode before the end is Arion's being thrown overboard. Apart from that, the entire libretto is written in Seth's trademark humorous and witty style. Even the dedication is characteristic:

For the wild dolphin, 'Fungie'

Irish dolphin, swift and single,
Dwelling off the coast of Dingle,
Choosing now and then to mingle
With the flipperless and glum,
Bringing wonder and elation
To our jaded human nation,
I present you this creation,
Of my fingers and my thumb.[6]

Seth evinces a remarkable imaginative faculty in the descriptions of the sea-world of dolphins. Harnessing scientific fact and historical folk-lore, he brings the world of dolphins alive before the eyes. The self-introductory song that the dolphins sing for Arion incorporates biological facts about dolphins into a witty song:

Fish give us sufficiency
Beneath the sea
As you can see.
We eat with great efficiency
Beneath the sea
As you can see.

. . . .

Our skins are smooth and rubbery,
Our bulky bodies blubbery
We harry herring happily
And swallow salmon snappily.
With unspecific gravity
And sinusoidal suavity

We harry herring happily
And swallow salmon snappily [...] (42-43).

It is a fact that dolphins exhibit a sense of humour, and there are several accounts of dolphins rescuing humans. All these facts are incorporated into a dolphin—masque performed for Arion by the dolphins. Seth makes the dolphin-world a fun place to be, where the dolphin exhibit humanoid traits and an intelligence that surpasses even that of humans.

Seth also displays admirable sentience. The song of Arion before he leaps into the sea is recreated with such empathy that it does not seem to be the fruit of a literary exercise:

I do not wish to die. I fear to die,
To sink in the refection of the sky,
At such a fearful depth to be alone,

To merge with shell and coral, slime stone,
By tentacles canvassed, by green fronds curled,
To drown myself in such a silent world [...] (35).

After the tragic finale, the libretto ends on a meditative note:

May music bind the sky, the earth, the sea
In tune, in Harmony.

Dark sea, protect all voyagers whose home
Rests in your ring of foam.

Warm earth, teach us to nourish, not destroy
The souls that give us joy.

Bright stars, engrave my dolphin and my lyre
In the night sky with fire (60).

This invocation assumes cosmic proportions as the elements are invoked to play their part in the circle of life and provide healing to the scarred soul of humanity. In folk-lore, the lyre represents the elements of fire,[7] therefore it is only appropriate that Arion should ask the stars to engrave his lyre and his beloved dolphin in the sky with fire, causing the northern constellation of Delphinus and Lyra to appear in the sky.

In this libretto, Seth proves yet again his ability to incorporate the elements of storytelling into rhyme. This ability for rhyme, both silly and otherwise, evinces not only Seth's passion for versification but also his supreme unconcern about his image as a 'serious' writer. Critics looking for a certain literary high-mindedness in Seth will be disappointed, because Seth is one of those few writers who write unselfconsciously. It takes courage to come down from the epic sweep of *A Suitable Boy* to the miniature scale of a libretto, but Seth happily does both, not only for the reader's pleasure but perhaps more importantly, for his own. The primary justification of all art being to provide pleasure, Seth passes with flying colours. One finds it hard not to agree with Daniel Johnson of the Times, who says, "I have little doubt that at the age of 41, Vikram Seth is already the best writer of his generation."[8]

III. *THREE CHINESE POETS*

Vikram Seth's stay in China shaped three of his books—*From Heaven Lake*, *The Humble Administrator's Garden*, and *Three Chinese Poets*, although the latter was written much after Seth's return from China. Seth, in the introduction to *Three Chinese Poets*, explains the impetus that led to its creation:

> Works in translation from languages I do not understand have had as deep an influence on my own writing as works I have read in the original. In some cases, the translations have so moved me that I have tried to learn the original language of the work. [...] This book is presented as a dual offering—as thanks to those three translators of one generation (Charles Johnston, Richard Wilbur, Robert Fitzgerald) who have meant so much to me, and as thanks to the three Chinese poets of another generation whose original poems have meant even more.[9]

This is the spirit in which the book has been offered to connoisseurs of poetry.

Chinese Poetry has a long, fruitful history, dating from the "Book of Songs," compiled more than 2500 years ago. The three coeval poets (Wang Wei, Li Bai, and Du Fu), are T'ang dynasty poets, a dynasty celebrated for its poets, as for its nurturing of poets and poetry. It was during the reign of the T'ang dynasty that poetry composition was introduced as a component of the "Chin-Shi" (civil service) examination, thereby institutionalizing the poetic arts.

The poetic forms that evolved were a variety of formal, and increasingly informal, poetic expressions of form and content. The standard verse form was the lü–shih, or regulated verse. This rigorous form consisted of eight lines, conceived as four pairs of couplets, with rhymes mandatory on the even numbered lines and optional on the first. The lines of each middle two couplets had, in addition, to be grammatically parallel: if line one of couplet two read adjective noun verb caesura noun verb (red sun falls, birds settle), then line two of the couplet also had to read adjective noun verb caesura noun verb (white clouds float, moon rises). The poem, which could use either five or seven character per line, had to observe strict tonal regulations, moreover, with the class of tone for every character in every line mandated by the form. Several different sets of tonal sequences were possible, but once one was chosen by a poet, he could deviate from it only at the risk of being found a tactless, undisciplined boor.[10] Two other verse forms were ku-feng and yuch–fu: both ancient styles that took new shape in the hands of these poets.

Li Bai or Li Po as he is called in earlier translations has an inseparable companion in Dù Fu (also known as Tu Fu). Arthur Cooper points out that Li Bai is Yin to Du Fu's Yang. He says:

> Li Po is the Taoist in this pair of poets, and his constantly recurring symbol is the refuted light of the moon and night; whilst Tu Fu is the Confucian who from early childhood made the Phoenix his symbol, the Fire Bird symbolizing the yang.[11]

Vikram Seth brings in Wang Wei to complete the triumvirate. The standard trichotomy of Wang Wei as Buddhist recluse, Li Bai as Taoist immortal and Du Fu as Confucian sage has been rejected by some critics as unsubtle and artificial, but it can act as a classifying approximation for those approaching Chinese poetry of this period for the first time. The centre of gravity of their work, the characteristic emphasis of their most characteristic poems, is distinct and individual.[12]

Indeed, Wang Wei's signature is aloneness, emptiness a retreat into quietness, nature, and Buddhism. Li Bai is a Taoist (a way which concerns the recognition and pursuit of fundamental harmonies in nature and the world). Li Bai writes like a Taoist in that he approaches things obliquely, and is content to evoke the expression of things of nature is his poetry. Ken Hope says of Li Bai, "There is in his poems the spontaneous unfolding, branching out, and release that the Taoists have perceived in Nature."[13] Du Fu's poetry is Confucian in spirit, centring as it does on practical affairs and the social sphere.

Seth brings these three contemporary poets to the reader in all their diversity, although there are some common sentiments among them: "[...] their appreciation of music, their acute perception of nature, their bent towards nostalgia."[14]

Three Chinese Poets can be considered to be a primer of sorts to Chinese Poetry of the T'ang dynasty. In the introduction, Seth goes to great lengths to furnish the social and political backdrop of the T'ang era, and the way in which the upheavals of the age were inevitably reflected in the work of these poets. He also successfully links each one's poetry to each one's individual way of life: Buddhism for Wang Wei, Taoism for Li Bai and Confucianism for Du Fu. It becomes evident that Seth places a high value on the task of the translator, and sets certain standards for him. In this respect Seth is the exact antithesis of Ezra pound, who though accredited with the distinction of being Li Bo's foremost translator is English, nevertheless takes liberties with the text. In this context Seth says:

> There is a school of translation that believes that one can safely ignore many of the actual words of a poem once one has drunk deeply of its spirit. An approximate rendering invigorated by a sense of poetic inspiration becomes the aim. The idea is that if the final product reads well as a

poem, all is well: a good poem exists where none existed before. I should mention that the poems in this book are not intended as transcriptions or free translations in this sense, attempts to use the originals as trampolines from which to bounce off on to poems of my own. The famous translations of Ezra Pound, compounded as they are of ignorance of Chinese and valiant self-indulgence, have remained before me as a warning of what to shun (xxiv-xxv).

Seth is thus more in kinship with the school that admits the primacy of the original and attempts fidelity to it. In *Three Chinese Poets* he has tried not to compromise the meaning of the actual words of the poems, though he admits he has often failed.

It is incontrovertible that there are non-translatable elements is both prose and poetry that make a verbatim rendering impossible. The non-translatable elements in the regulated verse form (lü-shih) are discussed by Seth in the introduction to *Three Chinese Poets*. These two non-translatable elements are: the so-called 'tones', and exact grammatical parallelism.

In classical Chinese, syllables—each exactly one written character long—were classified into tones depending on the direction of pitch of the sound, the meaning of the syllable depending on the pitch-direction. Seth says that, "the pattern of tones in the regulated octet set up expectations and provided musical satisfactions that are impossible to provide in a non-tonal language like English. This is a part of what is necessarily last in translation" (xxii).

About the other feature-exact grammatical parallelism, Seth writes:

> This parallelism within each of the second and third couplets is a particular pleasure of the Chinese regulated octet, but in my translations I have often let natural English syntax override strict parallelism in order to avoid what might otherwise emerge as a choppy or a rigid rendering (xxii).

Seth further says:

> Even in prose the associations of a word or an image in one language do not slip reading into another. The loss is still greater in poetry, where each word or image carries a heavier change of association, and where the exigencies of form leave less scope for choice and manoeuvre (xxv).

In Chinese poetry, the aforesaid difficulty is still greater, firstly because the two languages do not have a common linguist base, and secondly because in the words of Greg Whincup:

> Chinese poems are like a string of jewels. The jewels are Chinese characters, each of which represents a one—syllable word. These little word—jewels are hard and unchanging, but when they are translated in to English each one seems to have several different meanings.[15]

This assertion in borne out by the fact that different translations of the same poem often strike one as being different poems altogether, suggesting that Chinese poetry in susceptible to a variation in interpretation.

All these difficulties compounded together coalesce into a task of translation that calls for a literary Hercules, and Seth does not disappoint. Ken Hope himself a translator, says that this small anthology has been translated "exquisitely by Vikram Seth."[16]

In this work Seth proves yet again that he is not a slave of preconceived notions about what he should write. He does not let any image of himself as a writer stand in the way of future work. In this avatar as a translator he attempts successfully, not only to trans-literate, but perhaps more importantly, not to 'trans-create,' à la Pound. This is evident from the pains he take to explain his methodology, the sources he cites, the notes to some of the poems, and most of all by the fact that this anthology does not resemble his original poetry. The Chinese poetry he has read no doubt forms part of the poetic tradition he inherits, but even a cursory glance at both types of poetry will reveal that the two are the works of different spirits, separated by a world of time. Seth always remains acutely conscious of his task as translator, and effaces his own poetic persona to the utmost to achieve the high standard of fidelity to the original that this volume exhibits. He is altogether determined to open up this ancient tradition of poetry to the reader in as verbatim a rendition as possible. The book has been offered to connoisseurs of poetry in a spirit of thanksgiving for the pleasure Seth has received from reading works in translation, a pleasure he now wishes to reciprocate.

Separated as one is from these three poets by a gap of twelve hundred years and an alien milieu, Seth opens up their world to one in this remarkable trans-literation. It is in great measure due to Seth's extreme conscientiousness in translation that he succeeds in bringing home to the reader the delicate beauty of this ancient tradition of poetry.

IV. *BEASTLY TALES FROM HERE AND THERE*

This retelling of classical folk-tales from the world over was conceived in a spirit of pure fun. Seth tells the reader, in the introduction to *Beastly Tales*: "Because it was very hot in my house one day and I could not concentrate on my work, I decided to write a summer stay involving mangoes and a river."[17] One story led to another until ten of these beastly tales were born. The first two stories come from the Panchtantra, the next two from Chinese folklore, the next two from Greece, the next two from the Ukraine, and the final two are product of Seth's own imagination, from what he calls the 'Land of Gup.'

In these ten tales, familiar characters take their place beside unfamiliar ones, all sharing some common traits: they are all quirky, and each character parodies one or another human trait, whether good, bad, or ugly. The tales use a variety of verse forms with different rhyme schemes and varying stanza lines, in the tradition of La Fontaine.

The tales begin with a solid fabular background, but as the stories unfold the beastly characters inhabiting them display quasi-human traits that take the tales to a deeper level. Seth does not always furnish the tales with a moral, and this makes the world of his animals a realistic minor in which can be discerned the ironies inherent in human life: where the slow and steady does not always win the race. However, despite the non-fairytale-like atmosphere, the tales are a far cry from the Grimm Brothers' school of story telling. There is joy and fun within these tales; animal behaviour has been studied and delineated with an amused perception that stuns by its accuracy and imaginativeness. The rhymes glue the reader instantly, the stories unfolding almost without the conscious passage of time, which speaks volumes for Seth's adroit handling of the verse medium.

Apart from Seth's obvious literary expertise, the tales are lent added enchantment by an alteration in the traditional contents. Seth makes the tales his own, bestowing upon them his particular brand of contemporary experience, speech and idiom. Thus, though archaic, the tales become firmly entrenched in the modern day zeitgeist. They grow in stature as they address the dilemmas of modern man. And yet, and this is their salient feature, they still manage to stand on their own as fables per se, providing delightful reading purely for their own sake: witty, wise, amusing, enlightening, and intellectually stimulating all at once. With this collection, Seth has earned his place in the prestigious lineage of Longfellow and Poe.

The first tale, "The Crocodile and the Monkey," is one that no doubt calls forth the childhood memories of all Indian readers: the foolish and uxorious crocodile, his greedy wife, and the smart monkey. The story throws light on the unflattering side of the female character, when it is at its basest level, grasping and insatiable, and also on the power women are capable of wielding over men, not withstanding that they are generally known as the weaker sex. Apart from the levels on which the tale unfolds, it gives delight through its verbal rendition. About the crocodile, Seth says, "He would view with tepid eyes/Prey below a certain size" (1). The crocodile's wife calls him "Scalykins" (2), and the monkey gets away with his life when he tells the gullible crocodile about the tree-hollow where he keeps:

[...] Heart and liver when I sleep,

Half my brain, a fingernail,
Cufflinks, chutney, and spare tail [...] (5-6).

The story is an eons-old one, but in retelling it Seth has imbued it with a charm and polish that has left it the richer.

The second tale is "The Louse and the Mosquito," again from Indian folklore. A louse (appropriately titled 'Creep') lives with her extended family in a king's bed, the entire brood drinking the King's blood every night. Due to their refined technique of blood-sucking, they cause no pain or discomfort and have thereby escaped detection for three decades. One day a mosquito flies in through the window and Creep does not have the heart to turn him away—so she warns him that he may stay overnight and drink blood only when the king is fast asleep. However, the egocentric mosquito pays scant heed and bites the king too quickly. As all hell breaks loose and the louse and her family are found and killed, the mosquito escapes detection and flies merrily out the window.

The tale is an exercise in warning against the dangers of being too kind–hearted and in having a personality weak enough to be taken advantage of. The poem has been written in an ironical vein, describing the havoc that descends on the louse and her family stemming from the mosquito's actions, and the cold-blooded nonchalance with which the mosquito, unharmed, takes off on another adventure, callously unconcerned with his part in the tragedy. Such indeed are the ways of the modern world, where a good action is often repaid with thanklessness and oftentimes even grief.

The next two tales are taken from the fabular annals of China. "The Mouse and the Snake" is a short poem extolling fortitude and courage even in the face of sorrow and danger. Two mice are feasting on grain when a snake slithers up and swallows one of them. The other one evades the snake, and when the snake has crept into hole, the mouse bites into its tail until the snake is forced to spit out the dead mouse.

The poem is sombre but ends on a light note, with Seth introducing himself in the last stanza as the poet Chang, who has written the poem, noting tongue-in-cheek:

[...] Where in elegiac meter
He extols the snake-Defeater
And in couplets sad and stoic
Celebrate her acts heroic—
Acts that prove that shock and pain,
Death and grief are not in vain—
Which fine lines, alive or dead,
Neither of the mice has read (17).

The second poem from the Chinese is "The Rat and the Ox," dealing with that most famous of all Chinese things—the Chinese zodiac. The poem is remarkable for the ease with which Seth dons the mantle of story-teller: authoritative, amusing, witty, and erudite. In this poem Seth takes a sardonic look at the way governments work, both on celestial and earthly levels, and how decisions are often taken without proper research, due to the time-consuming process of data-collection.

The next two poems—"The Eagle and The Beetle" and "The Hare and the Tortoise" have Grecian origins. The former tells how a beetle avenges the death of its friend, the hare, which has been preyed upon by an eagle, Zeus' divine bird. The moral is crystallized by Seth himself in the final lines of the poem:

[...] But others, not so superstitious,
Merely assert that Fate's capricious,
And that the strong who crush the weak,
May not be shown the other cheek (31).

"The Hare and the Tortoise" shocks by its surprise ending, but the shock is quickly replaced by a recognition that this is truly the way the real world works; where slow and steady may win the race but not the crown, where flightiness and a devil–may-care attitude arc cn vogue; where it dull and stupid to be diligent and responsible, and hip to be inane. The hare is every inch the empty-headed but visually appealing socialite. The tortoise is an embodiment of all that is sober and serious in human nature; diligence, practicality, common sense. Each of them thinks the other one to be a perfect fool. Soon a race ensues to settle the tortoise's ancestral claim that he would win any contest between himself and the pompous hare. The tortoise does win the race but just when he is about to indulge in smug self-satisfaction for not being empty-headed like the hare, the hare steals the limelight by becoming the cynosure of all eyes, in spite of having lost the race. Her defeat is accepted by her admirers as evidence of her decadence, which is apparently something to enviously aspire for: "You have tendered gold and booty/To the shine of sleep and beauty" (40). Her defeat is glorified as "All the world lost for a snooze" (40). Seth portrays the irony of life, where the hare, despite losing the race, nevertheless steal the show. The description of the race conjures up images of movie stars, with all their airs and paraphernalia. There is satire in the narration of the hare selling book and movie rights, akin to the one-day wonders who get famous for notoriety and make hay while they are in the sun. The traditional fabular content is thus altered to place the tale in contemporary context. Seth even pauses to shock the tortoise out of his holier-than-thou air of superiority:

> [...] After the announcer's gun
> Had pronounced that he had won,
> And the cheering of the crowd
> Died at last, the tortoise bowed,
> Clasped the cup with quiet pride,
> And sat down, self-satisfied.
> And he thought: "That silly hare!
> So much for her charm and flair.
> So much for her idle boast.
> In her cup I'll raise a toast
> To hard work and regularity.
> Silly creature! Such vulgarity! [...]" (39).

However, the tortoise has barely caught its breath when the hare's reception far outshines his own, and he is ruthlessly sidelined: "Thus, the hare was pampered rotten/And the tortoise was forgotten" (41).

The next two poems—"The Cat and the Cock" and "The Goat and the Ram" are from the Ukraine. The former portrays the friendship between the cat and a cock and how the enterprising cat saves its foolish friend from being devoured by a fox. Seth makes the tale interesting by portraying the cat as a fiddler who knows his flats from his sharps, and the cock as an accomplished singer. The last paragraph is highly amusing in its portrayal of the way in which two friends raid the fox's larder and wreak havoc in her house before escaping. "The Goat and The Ram" shows how quick thinking can sometimes save one's life.

The last two poems came to Seth as he says 'directly from the Land of Gup.' It is a measure of Seth's talent that these two poems are far superior in content to the preceding fables. The first poem is a delicate satire on the ironies of life—where the untalented but loud mouthed and overbearing types dominate over the truly gifted, who are often unsure of their talent. The nightingale fails to recognize the beauty of her own song and loses her confidence totally when the frog tabulates her faults. The frog exploits her in the way modern art directors exploit fledgling artists—earning bushels of money off them and pretending that they are doing the artists a favour by deigning to notice them. The insensitive and brash attitude of the frog finally ends in the nightingale falling dead due to over-exertion. The frog, now with no one to out sing him, drones on unchallenged. The poem thus shows the evil in human nature—when a lesser talent, instead of trying to raise itself to the sublimity of the greater one, tries to drag the other down to its own base level in order to feel adequate.

"The Elephant and the Tragopan" is the final poem in this collection. It is quite a long poem, exploring in detail the plight of our animal brothers as they struggle, mutely, to exist in a world that is fast turning into a concrete jungle. Bingle Valley and its animal inhabitants represent all forest ecosystems around the globe that are endangered by the marauding tactics of man. The elephant sums up the threat that man constitutes to animals in the following words:

> [...] He sees this planet as his fief
> Where every hair or drop or leaf
> Or seed or blade or grain of sand
> Is destined for his mouth or hand.

If he is thirsty we must thirst—
For all creatures, man comes first.
If he needs room, then we must fly;
And if he hungers, we must die [...] (74).

And this is putting it mildly. The poem then takes a turn as the animals form a plan of action to save their valley. From this point on the poem clearly portrays the struggle between the ecologists, and animal rights groups and hard hearted politicians who left their consciences somewhere on the road to power and who are in charge of sealing such decisions as the damming of rivers and the cutting of forests. This last tale presents images of men in power, bureaucratic evasion and red tape, and the parasitic behaviour of politicians, thriving at the expense of the country's economy—all collectively resulting in corruption.

When the animals march in protest against the invasion of Bingle Valley, the 'Bigshot' [corrupt politician] attempts to bribe the elephant and later threatens to kill the cock if they do not sign over Bingle Valley to him. It is then that Bigshot's son—'Smallfry'—enters, as a shining ray of hope for the animals and their valley, chastising his father for being underhanded and selfish. Smallfry is on the animals' side, upholding their right to live in peace in their natural habitats. Bigshot is initially perplexed by this treason and says to his son —"Your education's made you weak/A no-good, nattering nature-freak [...]" (89).

The above lines state the viewpoint of the hardened older generation towards the new one, whose education teaches them to love, respect, and conserve Nature, not to loot and pillage her resources. However, the son is no match for the father and the tragopan is killed. Things grow complicated as the tragopan is immediately accorded the status of a martyr or war-hero, and the news of the struggle spreads like wildfire. The press make much of the story and it receives too much publicity to be conveniently swept under the carpet. Towards the end, Seth says that this is a tale without an overt moral but the perspective reader may discern several, two of which are: that one must continue doing one's work even against all odds, and the other that even in the face of adversity, someone will be there to provide courage and hope—"For Smallfry swim in every pond/Even the Doldrums of Despond" (93).

Seth deliberately leaves the question of the fate of Bingle Valley unanswered, because as he says:

> [...] The resolution of their plight
> Is for the world, not me, to write (93).

These are the ten poems constituting the collection. The tales all have familiar threads running through them, but their versification imbues them with an added charm that makes them irresistible. The lines follow smoothly, and one reads on in rapt attention as the stories unfold. Seth's polished humour lends the light touch. With their portrayal of human foibles in the guise of animals, these tales delineate the world as it is today; they make the reader stop for a moment and introspect; to reaffirm values. For those who do not wish to burden themselves with thinking, the tales provide great pleasure in their fabular context alone. This is the reason that *Beastly Tales* is for people ranging in age from eight to eighty, and Seth, predictably tongue-in-cheek, exhorts the reader to "enjoy them all and have a beastly time" (Introduction).

Notes

1. Kati Stammwitz, *Turning the Telescope in the other Direction: Four Interviews with Post–Colonial Travel writers*. URL:www.ph-erfurt.de/ neumann/eese/artic99/stamm/1-99.html
2. D. Maya,"Narrating the Self: Vikram Seth's 'From Heaven Lake' and Naipaul's 'Area of Darkness;'" *Comparative Indian Literature*, ed. C.K.Visweswara Rao and R.K. Dhawan, Prestige Books, New Delhi, 2001, 189.
3. *From Heaven Lake*, Chatto and Windus, Great Britain, 1983, 20.
4. Shakespeare *Twelfth Night* I.ii.17.
5. Regina Blackstock, "Dolphins and Man [...] Equals?" May 1970. URL:www.polaris.net/~rblacks/dolphins.htm
6. *Arion and the Dolphin*, Viking Penguin India, 1994.
7. Murray Hope, *The Ancient Wisdom of the Celts*, The Aquarian Press, London, 1987.
8. *From Heaven Lake*, from the back cover.
9. *Three Chinese Poets*, Viking Penguin India, 1992 ed., xiii.

10. J.P. Seaton and James Cryer, *Bright Moon, Perching Bird: Poems by Li Po and Tu Fu*, Middletown, Ct: Wesleyan University Press, 1987, xi-xii.
11. Arthur Cooper, *Li Po and Tu Fu: Poems Selected and translated with an Introduction and Notes*, Harmondsworth: Penguin Books, 1973, 18-19.
12. *Three Chinese Poets*, xvi.
13. Ken Hope, *Selected Poems of Li Bo in Different Translations*, URL:www.northshore.net/homepages/hope/Libointro.html
14. *Three Chinese Poets*, xv.
15. Greg Whincup, "The Heart of Chinese Poetry," New York, Anchor Books, 1987, 4.
16. Hope, *Ibid.*
17. *Introduction to Beastly Tales*, Viking Penguin, India, ©1991.

7

An Overview

After Rushdie had irreversibly redefined the parameters of the Indian novel in English with *Midnight's Children*[1] (1981), Indian writing in English underwent a long-overdue renaissance. Rushdie has to his indisputable credit the fact that he liberated Indian English writing from the baggage of imperial and colonial India. It has been a long road from the diffident, self-conscious, and apologetic style in which the earlier writers wrote to the privileged status Indian English writers now command.

Along with Rushdie, Seth has been hailed as the standard-bearer of Indian writing in English. These two are, by general consensus, considered to be in the vanguard of a group that is sometimes referred to as 'the-empire-writes-back' generation. But to circumscribe writers by any barriers is to limit the creative process, for in a world that has truly shrunk in space and time, the complex heterogeneity and multi locational contexts of Indian English writing totally subvert the borders erected by nationalism. It is now impossible to think of any Indian writer as belonging only to a national tradition, and equally impossible to limit the creative process by ascribing it within the matrix of a singular and insulated tradition. When Nobel laureate Sir V.S. Naipaul interrupted Nayantara Sehgal in mid-sentence, as she was expounding upon the reflections of colonialism in Indian literature, with, "Colonialism is over. Let's not be banal in our discussion,"[2] perhaps he was pointing out astutely a major lapse on the part of those writers who hammer on ad nauseam about colonialism and its repercussions, and equally on the part of those critics who regard works from previously colonised nations solely as cultural artefacts that hold the key to feelings of angst and oppression now being regenerated in their literature.

There is no doubt that it is a writer's prerogative to be nationalistic in theme if he or she so chooses, but to condemn a writer for being un-nationalistic is surely to miss the point. In the case of Indian English writers, 'Indian-ness' is certainly not indispensable to their writing. Expatriate Indian writers avoid the controversy due to their obvious and inarguable exposure to other cultures, but even in the case of those like Seth, who were born in India and spent some of their formative years here, it cannot be held against then that they are un-Indian, for with their trans-national mobility, the culture they inherit is a global culture that includes India but is not limited to it. Seth in particular cannot be clubbed willy-nilly with the other Indo-Anglian writers because firstly, he was never overly nationalistic in his writing to begin with, and secondly, for him India has not been the site for fashioning his identity as a writer. In these respects, as in several others, Seth is quite different from other Indian writers, for he demands no indulgence for being Indian, and he does not pander to the West's current penchant for lapping up Indian exotica. His work, therefore, cannot be evaluated on the basis of its 'Indian-ness,' for "he has no axe to grind about India, no thesis to argue,"[3] not even in a novel as Indian in theme as *A Suitable Boy*.

Contemporaneously Seth does belong to the post-colonial period, as also to the empire-writes-back-generation, but for what such distinctions are worth, his writing does not share the preoccupations of either. In his writing there is no angst, no complexes, no odes to the British Raj, no searching for an 'Indian' identity. His early poetry does betray a wistful loneliness, but it is for the home and family rather than for the familiarity of the native land. Even this feeling of uprooted ness is momentary, for apart from these early poems (as for instance, *Divali*), there is no trace of a hankering after roots in Seth's writing. In effect, Seth becomes confidently rooted in his rootlessness, turning his itinerant lifestyle into an asset rather than into a liability. His work epitomises the integration of an individual sensibility with the ethos of a global culture. Cultural displacement ceases to matter to him, as he assumes the role of the immigrant connoisseur who has mastered a world alien to him on his own terms, effectively colonising the fictional space of the West.

However, as a polymath, he is impossible to pigeonhole as a writer. What is certain is that his literary output is essentially an exploration of his immigrant experiences. The milieu Seth draws from is as wide and varied as his diverse geographical sojourns because he finds the world outside of India interesting enough to enable him to write more than just exilic versions of an India suffused with nostalgia and myth. His novels *The Golden Gate* and *An Equal Music* are instances in point. Such novels cannot be evaluated on the basis that they have been written by an Indian. They can be judged only on the basis of their literary quality and on the authenticity of the experience the writer has tried to communicate. It therefore becomes essential to disregard national barriers and view works in a non-national context in order to avoid the pitfalls inherent in judging by nationality as the sole criterion. In the case of Vikram Seth, it becomes essential that he be regarded purely as an artist, for the fact that he is an Indian is by and large incidental to his writing. In this context, Michel de Certeau's concept of Plural Culture,[4] as an ongoing struggle against the imposition of a hegemonic cultural norm, assumes great importance, for it enables the critic to pinpoint the factors that determine the evolution of an artist. Seth himself gets to the root of the debate when he says that the categories that writers are generally ascribed to, on the basis of themes and nationality are "fascinating but in the final analysis irrelevant."[5] The artistic process needs to be liberated from the aforesaid circumscriptions, if writers are to be true to themselves. In answer to how he sees himself Seth says:

> I see myself as Indian (even if I hadn't written *A Suitable Boy* this would be true), and primarily as a poet (seven of my books are in verse and the other two contain a fair

amount of it). But if tomorrow I were inspired to write a quintet of prose plays set in Iceland I would let neither image of myself stand in the way.[6]

Clearly, the answer to Seth's remarkable diversity of both apprehending and expressing lies in this attitude he holds towards the creative process. This tendency to be receptive to different experiences and suggestions would appear to serve the artist quite well. But the imagination needs something concrete to work upon, and in this respect Seth willingly obliges, leaving no stone unturned for his research on any aspect of his choice of theme. For *A Suitable Boy*, he devoted a year exclusively to research, and for *An Equal Music* he attended classes for the deaf, attended their music rehearsals, even lived with musicians, in order to apprehend to the utmost every aspect of his subject. In the hands of lesser artists, such painstaking research would appear contrived, but Seth uses his research to add depth to his stories and to add to the texture of his novels. The effect is verisimilitude, but verisimilitude judiciously supplemented by the artistic faculty.

Seth's artistic goals are remarkably like those of the Maggiore quartet he has written about, who spurn modern cacophony in favour of the Classics, even though the former is à la mode. William Sutcliffe points out, "Critics are blind to the labour and skill behind the flawless, transparent style of which Seth is a master."[7] His writing stands in sharp contrast to the involuted style that other modern writers who wish to be taken seriously adhere to, and which results from too much emphasis on stylistic devices. By his writing Seth has proved that it is not necessary to be obtuse in order to be appreciated.

Seth's gift is that he combines the sensitivity of a poetic soul with the narrative dexterity of a skilled raconteur. Also, he has this in common with the great writers of all time: his themes possess substantial value and a genuine human meaning, embracing life with all its passions, problems, and vicissitudes. Seth's literary output is supported by this ample knowledge of life. William H. Hudson states:

> Whatever aspects of life the novelist may choose to write about, he should write of them with the grasp and thoroughness which can be secured only by familiarity with his material.[8]

This particular quality is epitomised in Jane Austen (whom Seth acknowledges as a master), and adhered to by Seth, resulting in a fidelity to experience that accounts for much of the narrative hold that he wields over the reader, for he also possesses the artist's wonderful faculty of making the reader see and feel with him.

The philosophy that Seth presents in his novels is fresh and serious and is expressed with sufficient power to provide more than superficial entertainment for the idle hour. His works possess a significance that no thoughtful reader is likely to overlook. This is evident because in discussing any of his works one finds oneself discussing life itself. All art, dealing with man's actions in the world, becomes a criticism of life, and every author has values that may be inferred from his works. In the way that Shakespeare's work, though it had not been written with any express moral purpose in mind, nevertheless presents a compendium of observations that can be categorised as general truths, Seth's writing too reveals his thoughts about life, his moral codes. He has a holistic view of life, a hope for a humane and harmonious world. By the keenness of his vision, Seth sees the world as it exists, and it grieves him—but he cannot abandon the world, nor reject it, because he sees men and women essentially as they are: "foolish but kind, stupid, but human, and above all, capable of love."[9]

The salient feature of Seth's writing is that he is consistently true to the artistic process. He says that he tries to write as truly and literally as he can, and that no amount of persuasion from publishers to tailor bits of his work to suit a certain section would make him change it. It is a situation where he gains some readers and loses some, with each work. But for Seth the primary concern is to write, not to write with book sales and reviews in mind. He says, "After all, I am a poet. And that is a tiny audience,"[10] implying that it does not matter how large or how small his readership is, as long as the reader he addresses himself to, appreciates him. He says, "[...] Dear though the reader might be, I'd be silly to cater to what the reader wanted."[11] It is this fidelity to experience and to predilection that accounts for much of the pleasure in reading Seth.

His writing has received world wide acclaim, and in 2001 he was conferred the OBE (Order of the British Empire) for his services to literature, but with true artistic stoicism Seth asserts, "one shouldn't take the eulogies that one gets too seriously nor should one take the worst of the denigration, the truth is somewhere betwixt and between and you only do the beat you can."[12] And as every author knows, it is time, not a jury-board, that hands out the ultimate prizes. To be sure, readers will return to Seth whenever they wish to be drawn into a world where the author has tried to convey his vision of life as truthfully as possible, and commendably, has often succeeded.

On assessing Seth's literary achievement, it becomes evident that he cannot be compared to say a Rushdie or even a Naipaul for instance. This is because Seth's aspirations are very different. His intention as an author is never to be overbearing. Hè has no designs on the reader, no accusations to hurl, no expectations that the reader should read more into his work than the obvious. If any motive at all is to be ascribed to his writing it would be the pleasure principle of art. In addition, it cannot be emphasized enough that Seth's major achievement is the rejection of prevailing literary trends in order to return to that distant time when literature had appeal not only for the intellectual person but also for the average fiction reader. The modernist de-linking of what qualifies as literature with mainstream fiction is an abyss that Seth has adroitly bridged. By focussing on the simpler, universal passions, he addresses himself to readers irrespective of caste, creed or nationality, and more importantly, his lucid style makes his work very accessible to all readers. Readers can approach his work without feeling apprehensive about being subjected to the stylistic devices that often prove to be the bane of modern writing. With its wit, humour, and its keen sense of life, there can no doubt that his work exhibits a timeless quality that assures Seth his place in posterity.

Notes

1. Rushdie, *Midnight's Children*, Penguin, USA, 1991.
2. Nona Walia, "Some Scenes from a Literary Festival," *The Times* (Delhi), Feb. 25, 2002.
3. "As the Raj Turns —*A Suitable Boy* by Vikram Seth," *The New Republic*; Washington; Jun 14, 1993.
4. Michel de Certeau, *La Culture au Pluriel*, 10/18, Paris, 1974, 27, 299.
5. "Introduction to *The Poems* 1981-1994," Penguin Books India, 1995, xv.
6. *Ibid.*
7. William Sutcliffe, "*An Equal Music* by Vikram Seth," *The Independent*, (U.K.) Apr 4, 1999.
8. Hudson, William H. *An Introduction to the Study of Literature*, George Harrap and Co. Great Britain, 1910. 133.
9. Andrew H. Wright, *Materials and Themes, Jane Austen's Novels*, Chatto and Windus, Great Britain, 1953, 27.
10. Soumya Bhattacharya, "Amit Wasn't Suitable for Seth," *India Informer*, Calcutta, Dec. 13, 1999.
11. Akash Kapur, "The Seth Variations." *Atlantic Unbound Online Edition.* June 23, 1999.
12. *BBC News Online Edition.* "Vikram Seth Tells His Story." July 9, 1999.

Selected Bibliography

(A) WORKS BY VIKRAM SETH

Mappings (A collection of poems). Calcutta. Writers' Workshop, 1981.

From Heaven Lake (A travel book). Chatto and Windus, 1983.

The Humble Administrator's Garden. Carcanet Press Ltd. 1985.

The Golden Gate: (A novel in verse). Random House Inc. New York 1986.

All You Who Sleep Tonight (A collection of poems). Viking Penguin Ltd. 1990.

Three Chinese Poets (Translation). Faber and Faber Ltd. 1992.

Beastly Tales from Here and There (Collection of poems).Viking Penguin India Ltd. 1992.

A Suitable Boy: (A novel in prose). Viking Penguin India Ltd. 1993.

Arion and the Dolphin (An opera text). Viking Penguin India Ltd. 1994.

An Equal Music (A novel in prose).Viking Penguin India Ltd. 1999.

(B) INTERVIEWS

Alexander, Ruth and Isabella Pereira, *Dark Lord of the Seth*. *Cherwell* Online Edition. URL: www.planet-hardcore.de/cherwell/archive/ht00/3/features/6.html

BBC News Online Edition. *Vikram Seth Tells His Story*. July 9, 1999.

Bemrose, John. "Full Lotus Fiction—A Suitable Boy by Vikram Seth." Toronto: *Maclean Hunter Consumer Publications*. May 31, 1993.

Bryan, Sarah. "Author Seth Rhapsodizes on A String Quartet in His Latest Novel." *St. Louis Post Dispatch*. June 10, 1999.

Carey, Lynn. "Seth Draws On His Emotional Past to Create Characters." London: *Times Book Club* Interview. July 30, 2000.

Crowe, Sara. "No Ice, Vikram." *The University of Sydney News*. March 23, 2000.

Currie, Jay and Michèle Denis. "Hearing a Different Music." *January Magazine*. June 1999.

Gavron, Jeremy. "A Suitable Boy." *Daily Mail and Guardian* Online Edition. July 20, 1999.

Haven, Cynthia. "Poetic Licence." USA: *Stanford Magazine*. May/June 1999.

Kapur, Akash. "The Seth Variations." *Atlantic Unbound* Online Edition. June 23, 1999.

Kohli, Suresh. "Another Suitable Boy." *The Hindu* Online Edition. May 16, 1999.

Knorr, Katherine. "Vikram Seth Plays to His Truest Judges." *International Herald Tribune* Online Edition. Apr. 24, 1999.

Paul, Seema. *The Telegraph*: Calcutta. Feb. 21, 1993.

Rediff. com. "Writing Is a Big Risk." URL: www.rediff.co.in/therediffbooks.inter.html

Rediff.com. "The Vikram Seth Chat." URL: www.rediff.com/chat/vikcha.html

Roy, Amit. *The Telegraph*: Calcutta. Aug. 29, 1992.

Sharma-Jensen, Geeta. "Poetry or Prose, East or West, Seth Simply Follows His Muse." *Journal Sentinel* Online Edition. May 19, 2000.

Verghis, Sharon. "Symphony of Words From the Man Who Found A Beethoven Opus." *The Sydney Morning Herald*. Mar 14, 2000.

Verma, Pavan K. "Of Love, Loneliness, and The Fine Art of Storytelling." *The Hindustan Times*: Delhi. May 2, 1999.

Writers on Writing. Radio Series Transcript. Australian Broadcasting Corporation. URL: www.abc.net.au/writers/writesummary.htm

(C) CRITICISM ON VIKRAM SETH

Agarwalla, Shyam S. *Vikram Seth's: A Suitable Boy-Search For An Indian Identity*. Prestige Books: Delhi. 1995.

Blake, David, "Me And My Fiddle." *Al-Ahram Weekly*. 9-15 Sept. 1999.

Carey, John. "Review of An Equal Music." the *Sunday Times*, London, March 28, 1999.

Davie, Donald. Review of *The Humble Administrator's Garden*, Front Flap, Penguin India, 1994.

Desai, Anita. "Sitting Pretty." *The New York Review of Books*: New York. May 27, 1993.

Fausta. URL: www.barnesandnoble.com/bookshelf/fiction/best1.asp

Hollinghurst, Alan. "In The Onegin Line." the *Times Literary Supplement*, July 4, 1986.

Jacques, Leslie. "Rhyme and Reason," *Span*, Nov. 1986.

Jha, Ashok K. "Vikram Seth: the Golden Gate and Other Writings," *Recent Indian Fiction*, ed. R.S. Pathak, Prestige Books, 1994, 56.

Kapur, Akash. May 13, 1999. URL:www.salon.com/books/review/1999/05/13/seth/index.html

Karunakaran, Supriya. "Games The Novelists Play: The Subversive Rebellion of Vikram Seth in The Golden Gate." *Fiction of The Nineties*. Prestige Books: Delhi. 1994.

Kaul, A.N. "Wise and Witty." *Indian Literature-Sahitya Academy Bimonthly* no.132, July-August, 1989, 106.

Kennedy, X.J. URL: www.amazon.com

Lowe, Peter. "The Voice of The Turtle." URL: www.voiceoftheturtle.org/reviews/book/peter-seth.html

Maya, D. "Narrating The Self: Vikram Seth's From Heaven Lake and Naipaul's Area of Darkness." *Comparative Indian Literature*. Ed. C.K. Visweswara Rao and R.K. Dhawan. Prestige Books. 2001.

Morse, Ruth. "Rooted Cosmopolite: Vikram Seth and 'The Scars of Middlemarch.'" Fitzwilliam College, Cambridge. URL: www.perso.worldonline.fr/ebc/s.html.

Parks, Tim. "Sentimental Education." *New York Book Review*, July 15, 1999.

Patel, Devesh. "Poetry of an Exile." Contemporary Poetry Review. URL: www.webdelsol.com/CPR/Patel/ Vikram.html

Raghavan, Amit V. URL: www.emory.edu/ENGLISH/ Bahri/ Seth.html

Roy, Nilanjana S. "The Secret of Being A bore is to Say Everything." URL:www.indiawrites.com/archives.cfm?

Sutcliffe, William. "An Equal Music By Vikram Seth." *The Independent* Online Edition. Apr. 4, 1999.

Towers, Robert. "Good Enough for Her Mother's Mother's Mother," *New York Times*, May 9, 1993.

Vijaysree, C. "Vikram Seth." *Writers of The Indian Diaspora*. Ed. Emmanuel S. Nelson. Greenwood Press: Westport, CT. ©1993.

Worth, Robert. "India—All of it—A Suitable Boy," *Commonweal Foundation*, May 21, 1993.

Yardley, Jonathan. "A Dickens for the Subcontinent," the *Washington Post*, 25 April, 1993.

D. GENERAL REFERENCE WORKS

Anand, Mulk Raj. *The Private Life of an Indian Prince*, London, Hutchinson, 1963.

Barret Browning, Elizabeth. *Aurora Leigh*.

Berger, Melvin. *Guide to Chamber Music.* Great Britain: Robert Hale Ltd. ©1985.

Blackstock, Regina. "Dolphins and Man...Equals?" May 1970. URL:www.polaris.net/~rblacks/dolphins.htm

Byron, *Don Juan.*

Cooper, Arthur. *Li Po and Tu Fu: Poems Selected and translated with an Introduction and Notes*, Harmondsworth: Penguin Books, 1973, 18-19.

de Certeau, Michel. *La Culture au Pluriel*, 10/18, Paris, 1974, 27, 299.

El Pequeno Larousse Ilustrado, 469, 1996 ed.

Forster, E.M. *Aspects of the Novel*, Penguin Books, 1927, 74.

Gioia, Dana. "Can Poetry Matter?" *The Atlantic Monthly*; May, 1991; Volume 267, no. 5; 94-106.

Hofstadter, Douglas. "What's Gained in Translation." ©*The New York Times Company.*

Holland, Bernhard. *New York Times,* n.d.

Hope, Ken. "Selected Poems of Li Bo in Different Translations," URL: www.northshore.net/homepages/ hope/Libointro.html

Hope, Murray. *The Ancient Wisdom of the Celts*, The Aquarian Press, London, 1987.

Hudson, William H. *An Introduction to the Study of Literature*, George Harrap and Co. Great Britain, 1910. 321.

Malgaonkar, Manohar. *The Princes*, Orient Paperbacks, New Delhi, 1963.

Pushkin, *Eugene Onegin.*

Rushdie, Salman. *Midnight's Children*, Penguin, USA, 1991.

Rushdie, Salman. *The Ground Beneath Her Feet*, New York: Henry Holt and Company, 1999.

Seaton, J.P. and James Cryer. *Bright Moon, Perching Bird: Poems by Li Po and Tu Fu*, Middletown, Ct: Wesleyan University Press, 1987, xi-xii

Shakespeare, *Twelfth Night* I.ii. 17.

Stammwitz, Kati *Turning the Telescope in the other Direction*: Four Interviews with Post-Colonial Travel writers. URL: www.ph-erfurt.de/~neumann/eese/artic99/stamm/1-99.html

Sullivan, J.W.N. *Beethoven, His Spiritual Development*, Vintage Books (A Division of Random House), New York, 1960, 4, 6.

Towne, A. "Homosexuality in American Culture," *American Mercury*, August 1951, LXXIII, 3-9.

Trilling, Diana "The Image of Women in Contemporary Literature," *The Woman in America*, ed. R.J. Litton, Boston, Houghton Mifflin, 1965, 61.

Whincup, Greg *The Heart of Chinese Poetry*, New York, Anchor Books, 1987, 4.

Wright, Andrew H. *Materials and Themes*, Jane *Austen's Novels*, Chatto and Windus, Great Britain, 1953, 27.

(E) GENERAL STUDIES ON INDIAN ENGLISH WRITING

Bengali, Shashank. "The Time is Right for Midnight's Children." *Knight Ridder Newspapers* Online Edition. July 9, 2000.

Bhatia, Nandi. "Indo-Anglian Writing." *Himalya Magazine* Online Edition. August 1999.

Burns, John F. "The People's Raj." *The New York Times* Online Edition. Oct. 12, 1997.

Gandhi, Leela. "Indo-Anglian Fiction: Writing India, Elite Aesthetics, and the Rise of the Stephanian Novel." *Australian Humanities Review*. 1997.

India Today Magazine, "The Empire Writes back," URL: www.india-today.com

Iyenger, K.R. Srinivas. *Indian Writing in English*. Sterling Publishers Pvt. Ltd., New Delhi.

Joshi, K.N. and B.S. Rao. *Studies in Indo-Anglian Literature*: Prakash Book Depot, Bareilly 1984.

Kalinnikova, Elena J. *Indian-English Literature: A Survey*. Ghaziabad: Vimal Prakashan, 1982.

Kohli, Devindra. "Tragic Love Affair? The Contemporary

Indian English Literary Scene." *Aspects of commonwealth Literature*: Vol. 1 (Oct. 1988—June 1989).

McCutchnion, David. *Indian Writing in English*. Calcutta: Writers' Workshop, 1969.

Mishra, Pankaj. "Midnight's Grandchildren." *Prospect Magazine*. Apr. 1997.

Naik, M.K. *A History of Indian English Literature*: New Delhi. Sahitya Academy, 1992.

N.E. Barucha and Vilas Sarang. *Indian English Fiction: An Assessment*. B.R. Publishing Corporation: Delhi, 1994.

Nemade, Bhalchandra. "Modern Indian Fiction: A Clear Case of Accultration." *Critical Responses to Commonwealth Literature*. Sterling Publishers: Delhi. 1993.

Nicholson, Kai. "Are We Expatriates?" *Commonwealth Writing: A Study in Expatriate Experience*. Ed. R.K. Dhawan and L.S.R. Sastry.

Pathak, R.S. *Recent Indian Fiction*: Prestige 1994.

Prasannarajan, S. "Imagining India—A Midnight Reading." ©1997 *Indian Express* Newspapers (Bombay) Ltd.

Sen, Sudeep. "Literature: Now it's The Empire Writing Back." *The Financial Times* Online Edition. Aug. 1, 1997.

Rushdie, S. and West, E. (ed.) 1997, *The Vintage Book of Indian Writing: 1947-1997*. Vintage, London.

Verghese, C. Paul. *Essays on Indian Writing in English*, N.V. Publications, Delhi, 1975, 47.

Walia, Nona. "Some Scenes from a Literary Festival," the *Times* (Delhi), Feb. 25, 2002.